D1558717

# *Rock n' Roll'n ~ The 50's & 60's*

## Jim Orr

Palmetto Publishing Group
Charleston, SC

*Rock n' Roll'n ~ The 50' s & 60's*
Copyright © 2019 by Jim Orr

napavalleytour@sbcglobal.net

# See Authors Artwork at :
# www.napavalleytourmap.com

All rights reserved
No portion of this book may be reproduced, stored in a retrieval system, or transmitted in any form by any means—electronic, mechanical, photocopy, recording, or other—except for brief quotations in printed reviews, without prior permission of the author.

First Edition

Printed in the United States

ISBN-13: 978-1-64111-342-7
ISBN-10: 1-64111-342-1

# CONTENTS

## THE ROCK n' ROLL 50's AND 60's

# *ACKNOWLEDGEMENTS*

Appreciation is extended to the Vallejo, California Naval and Historical Museum during the initial research on this book. I also thank my daughter Kelly, without whose help and devotion the production of this book would not have been possible.

When I first visited the museum, I suddenly realized the Vallejo Police Department was located in the same building fifty-nine years earlier. At that time, as noted in chapter 33 ( "The Party, the Shotgun Blast, the Stockade" ), under much direr circumstances, I walked up the same cold steps under the same dramatic chiseled axiom embedded in marble above the door: Theorized by Herodotus, the ancient Greek historian, 485 BC – c. 425 BC.

"THOUGH FREE, THEY ARE NOT ABSOLUTELY FREE, FOR THEY HAVE A MASTER OVER THEM, THE LAW."

# ADDITIONAL ACKNOWLEDGMENTS
## *Photos and Graphics*

Appreciation is extended to the following for use of photos or graphics:

---

Vallejo, California Naval and Historical Museum

Cover Photo:
Courtesy of the Estate of Jules Aarons and Gallery Kayafas
Copyright: © Estate of Jules Aarons

classicstock.com:
Vintage Image Resources ~ Kids playing marbles in 1950's,
Kids fishing, Book back cover photo

Barrett Jackson:
media@barrett-jackson.com - Classic Car Photo's

Bo Insogna - Striking Photography - Striking-Photography.com
bo@striking-photography.com - Old West Jail House

Phils Old Radios, http://antiqueradio.org/. Copyright 2018

At the movies - Ames Tribune photo
Courtesy Ames Historical Society
© Ames Tribune - All Rights Reserved

---

Additional artwork and graphics by author / artist Jim Orr

To my wife Joan of over fifty years, whose love of God helped her endure the many trials I've caused over those years.

To my daughter Kelly, without whose help this book could not have been printed.

To my son Toby and his family, who prayed for me while I was experiencing a long-term serious health issue during the writing of this book.

And . . . above all, to God, for helping me complete the book. Glory and honor to him!

# ABOUT THE AUTHOR

Jim Orr was born in upstate New York in 1940. He grew up in Vallejo, California during the fabulous *Rock n' Roll 50's & 60's.*

He holds a degree in Health Science from San Francisco State College and also attended graduate school at Golden Gate College. A graduate of the Santa Rosa School of Nursing, he worked as a Psychiatric Nurse for the California Department of Mental Hygiene and served in the Army Nurse Corp during the Vietnam War where he met his wife Joan who was also an Army Nurse.

Upon finishing his military service, Jim left the Nursing Profession to become a Deputy Probation Officer with the Solano County Probation Department. He ultimately attained an administrative position with that agency, having his office in Vallejo, California.

The author is also a well known Napa Valley Wine Country Artist. His artwork can be viewed at www.napavalleytourmap.com. He has also conducted private wine tours in that famous wine region and is the author of the travel book, *A Day or Two in The Napa Valley*. Jim has worked in many different professions, but regrets not having tried his luck at three others; a Geologist, a Stand Up Comic, and a Weight Guesser in the Circus!

# PRELUDE AND
# NOTES TO THE READER

During the planning of this book, I wanted its main theme to be about growing up and experiencing the exciting *American Graffiti* times during the *Rock n' Roll* 50's and 60's. However, I also felt compelled to include some information relative to my early years during the post-war 40's and early 50's preceding the *Rock n' Roll* era. I've also included some information relative to the post-60's days as well, closing out the book where I'm presently at in my life. In this regard, the book is separated into three main categories: The Early Years; The *Rock n' Roll* 50's and 60's; The Later Years.

I fully realize many readers may not really be interested in my early childhood years. Clearly understood. They certainly weren't boring, and you may find some of the stories very comical and entertaining. Laugh therapy's a good thing . . . right? In fact, I'll bet some of your own childhood experiences were similar to mine. The times may have been different, but we were all kids. Each of us still has those locked in memories of our bygone days, many good, some bad, yet still experiences that molded the fabric of our lives.

However, if you're not into reading about my Early Year experiences, simply skip over to *THE ROCK n' ROLL 50's & 60's* in Chapters 19 through 33 where the *"Real Meat"* of that period is covered.

# INTRODUCTION

In 1944 my parents decided to yank up their New York roots, pack up my younger brother Jerry and I in the old Chevy, and head to California. Many did the same during the waning days of World War ll, making a beeline to the Golden State hoping for a better life. The journey across country was fraught with many trials and tribulations: sleeping on the side of the road, constant car troubles, numerous delays, an accident, plus other problems a four year old could never clearly understand. After the long two-week journey, we finally arrived in Vallejo, California, the home of Mare Island, the first Navy shipyard on the West Coast. *The Yard*, as it was called, provided plenty of wartime job opportunities.

My dad got a job there, and we ended up living in Vallejo for many years thereafter. Much of the fun I had writing this book was remembering and reliving all the great adventures I had as a kid right up through the fabulous *Rock n' Roll* 50's and 60's, even laughing out loud on many occasions while writing about them. However, there was some sadness regarding the fading memories of those former times. Unfortunately, the fast-paced smart phone young people today will never clearly understand what they missed. The *Rock n' Roll* 50's and 60's were the best of times! Each of my experiences and adventures described occurred exactly as written. The story begins as my family embarks on the long journey across country from New York to California.

*Westward ho!*

# THE EARLY YEARS

## Chapter 1

## *WESTWARD HO!*

### New York to California

I've always enjoyed exploring new things; taking risks, climbing down a deep canyon to see what was there, fishing or panning for gold in a clear remote mountain stream, or taking a flyer at a new start up gold mining venture in Nevada. I even made an extensive attempt at becoming an artist, resulting in some limited success. Then there was that short stint as a wine tour guide in California's famous Napa Valley. Must have inherited some type of risk-taking gene from my dad, although most risks he took usually ended in disaster, as did many of mine. Like father, like son, I guess. We've all taken some risks in our lives, but my folks giving up everything in 1944 to travel three thousand miles from New York to California not knowing what was waiting? I guess that might qualify as a big-time risk. Many did the same in those days, pulling up roots and heading to the Golden State for their piece of the American Dream.

## Smoke under the hood, the accident : Onward Ho!

As we slowly trekked across country, I'd often see smoke coming from under the hood of the old Chevy. My dad would then pull over, get out, grab a large canvas bag hanging from the bumper, lift up the hood, then pour water into something he called the radiator. Then off we'd go until the car heated up again, repeating the same episode over and over across the United States.

## Winter: The rugged Sierra Mountains

After lumbering across the barren wastelands of Nevada, we finally reached the base of the rugged Sierra Nevada Mountains. Onward and upward we struggled that winter on old Highway 40. I remember my fingers sticking to the ice-cold window when I touched it. Then suddenly, a loud *BANG!* and a crash! I was now stuck under the front driver's seat, crying and in pain. I hear lots of noise, screaming, then more crying. The car had skidded off the road and hit something. Next thing I remember is my folks prying me out from under the seat, dusting me off, then "wagons ho" again toward the Promised Land.

## Constant quarrels

I also remember another unpleasant occurrence: my mom and dad arguing all across country. It continued throughout their lifetime. I felt very hurt by it. When it happened in the car, my way of escaping was to cower down in the back seat, covering my ears in an effort to avoid the noise. When it occurred in the home, I'd run and find a place to hide for some comfort. But there was no real escape. I'm certain most of the arguing resulted from my dad's drinking problem. He apparently wasn't always like that. Somehow it just happened along the way. He failed at much of what he tried in life. Maybe that was the reason. Even as an adult, I still get a knot in my stomach when I hear people around me arguing and screaming at each other, especially in front of their children.

# Chapter 2

## *ARRIVAL IN VALLEJO*

## Chabot Acres Housing Project

After the two-week journey, we finally arrived in Vallejo, California, a small town just north of San Francisco. We didn't have a place to stay, so we ended up sleeping on the floor of some Post 104 American Legion Hall. Shortly after, my folks met a nice family who let us stay in their home temporarily. We then moved to Chabot Acres, a low-rent housing project just outside town. Each house in Chabot was close to its neighbors, most being attached to each other. This closeness helped foster lasting friendships. Everyone helped each other and we rarely locked our doors. I remember going into my house never having to use a key. Just open the door, and in you go. The majority of people living in Chabot were African American, with some Caucasians, Mexicans, and a few other ethnic groups. As kids, we all got along fine, played together, had fun, and became close friends.

**Corner house on right in Chabot where I grew up as a kid**

## The dry salami and the .38 revolver

My dad's first job was a bartender at a local tavern. I recall two things about that job, one good, one bad. One night he came home with a long round thing in a package called a dry salami. He gave me and my brother a piece. Man, that was the best thing I'd ever tasted! On another occasion he came home mad as hell after being fired at the same tavern.

I remember him screaming at my mom while waving his .38 revolver in the air, threatening to go back and kill the owner. It never happened, but the incident painted a traumatic impression in my mind. I never forgot it. As I said, one good memory, one bad.

## Mare Island: First Navy shipyard on the West Coast

The next job my dad got was as a machinist at Mare Island Naval shipyard, the first Navy shipyard on the West Coast. Years later, my brother also ended up working at *The Yard* for his entire career. *The Yard* employed a large percentage of the population in Vallejo. However, President Bill Clinton shut it down in 1996. The closing of the shipyard had a lasting negative effect on the city for many years thereafter.

# Chapter 3

# *TIME TO GET LITTLE JIMMY IN SCHOOL*

## Catholic school: My first and last day!

My folks were Catholic, so when I was old enough, they decided to enroll me in this Catholic elementary school in the town of Benicia, about thirty minutes away from Vallejo. Never could figure out why they wanted me to go to school that far out of town. One thing for sure though, they didn't have a clue about what was to happen to their little Jimmy on his first and "last day" in Catholic Elementary School!

Here's a simple question: What does your average five year old know about being a Catholic? The answer? Nothing! All I remember is going to church, listening to some foreign language, and watching my mom and others play with beads and light candles. We also met a lot of women dressed in black, and we couldn't eat meat on Friday. Even as teenagers, my brother and I were forced to go to church, and once a week to confession. I remember going into the confessional booth, sitting down, then making up sins to confess to the priest just to get out of the place. I always believed in God, just not all the Catholic rituals, customs, and ceremonies.

So one Monday morning my folks drive me to Benicia to enroll me in this place called St. Dominic's. We went in, and I'm introduced to this woman dressed in black. Looking down at this five year old who'd rather be someplace else, she say's "Welcome to St. Dominic's, Jimmy. You're going to love it here." In response to her kind greeting, I'm certain I was thinking, "Don't bet on it, sister!" After all the initial introductions and formalities, my folks burned rubber back to Vallejo, my mom waving bye bye as the old Chevy disappeared in a cloud of dust. It almost seemed like they were happy to leave me there. As they were leaving, I swear I heard them both singing, "Hallelujah, hallelujah, free at last!" as they rocketed over the horizon. Ever feel abandoned? Man, were they in for a big surprise. "Hey, I don't like this place, I don't want to be here. Come back!"

After eventually calming down, I was taken to this sterile, cold classroom where another woman dressed in black looked down at me and said, "Welcome to St. Dominic's, Jimmy. You're going to love it here." After a couple hours in the *Inner Sanctum*, it was finally lunch time. In those days most kids had these square tin lunch boxes with neat pictures of cowboys and indians or ocean liners painted on them. Mine had a picture of the famous cowboy Roy Rogers and his horse Trigger. So I got my lunch box from the storage room fridge and went outside to enjoy my peanut butter and jelly sandwich, chocolate chip cookie, milk, and an apple. With no friends, I sat down alone next to a tree. Couldn't wait to dive in and enjoy the first bright spot of the day. Quickly opening my lunch box, I reached in, and guess what? It was *filled with ants!* "I want my mommy!"

After being reported missing in action, the nuns eventually found me outside crying hysterically, my Roy Rogers lunch box and food strewn all over the place, covered with ants. After a long failed attempt at trying to calm me down, one of the nuns finally decided to call my folks. As I was sitting in her office covered with tears, she got my mom on the phone and said, "Mrs. Orr, there's been a slight incident with your son here at school. Nothing serious, but I think its best you come pick up little Jimmy and take him home. I don't think he likes it here." My first and last day at Catholic Elementary School!....*Hoorah!*

# Chapter 4

# *GOTTA FIND*
# *A NEW SCHOOL FOR THE KID!*

## Everest Elementary

After being catapulted out of Catholic elementary school, my folks had to get me into someplace, so they enrolled me in Everest Elementary School back in Chabot, only four blocks from our house. I could then easily walk back and forth to school with all the other kids. Allowing a five year old to walk to school alone today would normally be out of the question. However, back in those days it was the norm. All the kids walked to school together. There was never the extent of weird stuff going on then that occurs today.

## Epilepsy: What's that?

Everest was a fun place to go to school, but I do remember one vivid event in kindergarten that really shook me up. I can still hear the loud, grimacing cries from the boy lying on the floor as he shook all over, this white stuff coming from his mouth. Our teacher told us to stay seated as she ran to him and put something in his mouth. After a short time, the violent shaking subsided and the boy sat up. Another woman dressed in white then came in and escorted him out. A while later he returned happy as ever, as if nothing had happened.

I'd never seen anything like that. It scared the crap out of me. I finally learned Billy had what was called epilepsy. Without warning, he would have these spontaneous spasms or seizures. After that, when it happened it was no big deal. We all knew Billy could have what us kids called the "Fits" at any time. He was a neat kid, and we all liked him a lot.

## Bullied at school: Never again!

Ever been bullied? I remember being bullied in school. Today, we hear about bullying all the time; bullying in the classroom, on the Internet, at the mall, in the grandstands, or at the workplace. Sadly, many kids have even taken their lives as a result of being bullied. So there was this brat at my school known to be the class bully. He usually sat behind me, and was always doing crazy things in class or making fun of others. One day while sitting behind me, he let out this huge fart. Everyone in class, including the teacher, heard it. After igniting this mammoth armor-piercing explosion, he immediately pointed to me and said, "Jimmy did it!" The entire class then began laughing at me. "Hey, I didn't do it! It was Robert!" But it was too late. The damage was done.

## "And the guy behind you won't leave you alone!"

In the 50's, Chuck Berry was the real king of *Rock n' Roll*. One of his popular songs was "School Days." You can check out where to listen to it later in the book. One of the lyrics in the song was, *"And the guy behind you won't leave you alone!"* These lyrics apply perfectly to the following incident with this brat Robert.

We were taking a quiz one day in class. Robert began tapping me on the back, trying to get the answers. I kept telling him to quit, but he wouldn't leave me alone. After school, he threatened to beat me up if I didn't help him in the future. Not long after, we were having another quiz. Robert started tapping me on the back again. This time I got really angry, stood up, and for the first time, confronted him in front of the teacher and the entire class. The teacher then disciplined him, although as usual, he denied doing anything.

That same day he followed me home. I knew he was going to beat me up, and although he was much bigger, I decided not to take it anymore. I noticed a long two-by-four board close by. I picked it up, walked over to him, and said, "Robert, leave me alone, or I'll bust you over the head with this!" He never bothered me again.

Interestingly, as Robert and I grew older, we would spend time together on occasion, and were even on the same school basketball teams. There was also another good result from my standing up to him. I never allowed anyone to ever bully me again!

# Chapter 5

# *GROWING UP IN THE PROJECTS*

## New Idea and Affordable!

Chabot Acres was a great housing project to grow up in. The idea was new, and the rent was affordable for those with little money. All the homes were built the same: small and square, with two or three bedrooms. In fact, everything in Chabot Acres was square with flat roofs; the homes, elementary school, local food market, stores, project maintenance building, everything. However, one thing for sure. Even though we were all basically poor kids growing up in square houses, we weren't square. We thought we were really cool!

## The Early Years: Hikes and rock fights

As kids, we couldn't wait to get up each morning in the summer and on weekends, and run out the door! Too much fun to be had. A hike with the gang to some far off secret place, or what about a friendly rock fight between your gang and the gang up the block? Get your team together, go out in the field, line up in the trenches across from one another, get your stash of dirt rocks ready, blow the whistle, then let 'em fly! No one ever got hurt that bad. Just make believe war games between two gangs. Plenty of other things to do as well. No sitting around wasting time, texting on handheld devices, or playing video games in those days. Too much fun to have!

## Baseball in the dirt field below Tank Hill

No manicured grass fields in those days. Just a dirt field out back of our house. Get all the gang together, choose up teams, then go out and set up the field. We used anything we could find for bases; old rags, cardboard, whatever. Then we let her rip, and played all day.

Our gang spent many days playing baseball or having rock fights out in the dirt field behind our house. The three tanks on the hill supplied water to the housing project. We'd often ride our go carts down the hill, or slide down the dry grass on it during hot summer days.

## Ever have a dog when you were a kid?

We had this dog when I was young, some kinda mutt, built low to the ground for speed. He loved playing a game of hide and seek. He would run and hide in the house, then wait for us to find him. Once we found him, he would go hide again. He'd play the game over and over if we'd let him. His name was Chongo. Never knew what his name meant, so I looked it up once. "Chongo: A Mexican dessert made with milk, sugar, and cinnamon." My folks weren't Mexican, so why they named him that, I'll never know. He would get so excited when we finally found him hiding behind the sofa or under the bed, then off he'd go and hide again.

Ever have a dog when you were a kid?

## M. P. Elston, M.D - "Time for another Penicillin shot!"

The closest medical facility to our home in Chabot was Kaiser Hospital, about 5 miles away. But, as unbelievable as it may seem today, we had a family physician who would actually "come to our house" when my brother and I were ill. His name was Dr. M.P. Elston. He was a kind, gentle, caring man who would arrive any time of the day or night to treat our maladies. He always carried a "Black Bag" filled with medical equipment, first aid supplies, tongue depressors, drugs, and…. hypodermic needles! In those days, the miracle antibiotic drug Penicillin was used routinely for most colds, flu, and other related illnesses, although it had little effect on "viral" infections. So, as it was on many "late night" occasions, Dr. Elston would arrive at our house, examine my brother or me, then pull out the dreaded "hypodermic needle" from his "black bag"…. "Time for another Penicillin shot!"

# Chapter 6

## *PLAYING MARBLES WITH THE GANG*

### Don't lose those shooters!

Our gang played marbles all the time. We all had our bags of color-ful marbles; glassies, cats eyes, swirls, rainbows, and all kinds of agates, but the ones we cherished the most were our shooters. We'd all go out in a dirt field, clean off a flat piece of ground, then draw a circle about four feet in diameter. Each kid had to throw three or four marbles in the circle from his or her stash, but never any of their favorite shooters. We'd then draw straws to see who shot first. The trick was to take one of your shooters, put it between your thumb and index finger, then launch it into the circle, hoping to hit one or more of the marbles inside.

Anything hit had to go outside the circle. Your shooter also had to stay inside to get another turn. If that happened, you got to keep the marbles hit outside and continue shooting. As long as your shooter stayed in the circle and you kept hitting marbles out, you kept playing. However, if your shooter bounced out of the circle without knocking any others out, it was the next kid's turn.

One other important rule about our game of marbles. If your shooter stayed in the circle, and no other marbles were hit out, it remained in the circle and was fair game for the next kid up. Lost a lot of good shooters in those days! The game went on until all the marbles in the circle were gone, or the gang decided to play another.

# Chapter 7

## *FIRST TV IN THE NEIGHBORHOOD*

### The One-Eyed Monster: "What's that?"

In the early 50's, we got the first TV in the neighborhood. Most couldn't afford one, but somehow my folks found a way to get it. It was a Hoffman brand, with a very small green screen. All the gang flocked over to our place to watch it. There wasn't much on in those days, but watching anything was fun. It was a new and exciting experience. The first thing to do was set it up. An antenna had to be placed on the roof to pick up the TV signal.

It was an erector set-looking device with long metal protruding arms. With the antenna secured to the roof, a long wire was then strung down through a window and hooked to the back of the TV. It was then ready to turn it on and *Rock n' Roll!*

## Back up on the roof: "Move that antenna!"

The first thing appearing on the screen was a test pattern image, usually the picture of an Native American with a large beautiful feathered headdress. If focused correctly, a knob on the TV was then turned to select a channel. Not many channels in those days, and no remote control devices. If the picture was blurry or snowy, one of us had to climb back up on the roof and move the antenna back and forth to catch the TV signal. As the antenna was turned, someone downstairs would yell out, "Turn it a bit to the left! Now a bit to the right! Okay, that's got it!" At other times, just banging on the side of the TV brought the picture in. Some TV's also came with a small antenna called "rabbit ears" that sat on top of the TV, but they never worked very well.

## Limited programs

The TV programs were limited, but who cared. Even the test pattern was fun to watch! I still remember all of us sitting around glued to the postage stamp screen, hypnotized by this box in front of us. There were programs such as Buffalo Bob, and his puppet Howdy Doody; Gene Autry cowboy westerns; Chet Huntley and David Brinkley news broadcasts; outer space Flash Gordon serials, mysteries, and a few others. When the TV signal was lost again, or the picture became snowy, the same ritual was repeated. Back up on the roof to adjust the antenna, or begin performing the highly technical procedure of banging on the side of the TV over and over in an effort to recover the picture.

Now and then, a small TV tube inside the device would blow out. My brother or I would then be sent down to the local TV shop at the *Big Store* to buy another. At times the large picture tube would also blow out. If that went, you had to go to the bank to get another!

# Chapter 8

# *FUN UP ON TANK HILL*

## Tank Hill: Up in flames!

Behind our house was a steep hill with three large tanks on it that supplied water to the complex in Chabot. Everyone called it *"Tank Hill."* In the hot summer, the grass on it became bone dry. One day three of us kids found a book of matches. After a long serious discussion about what to do with them, we finally decided to do the prudent and responsible thing: "Play with 'em!" My brother Jerry said, "Hey, let's light up that small patch of grass over there to see what happens!" So we sat down next to the hill and started lighting a patch. Light the grass, blow it out. Light it again, then blow it out again. "Man, this is fun!" Light it again. "Hey, where'd that wind come from? Quick, blow it out!" Too late, now the whole damn hill is on fire! We run like hell, and climb a tree. This man then comes, looks up, and say's, "I saw you kids start that fire!" "No sir, we've been up in this tree all day long!"

Finally, the fire trucks arrived, put out the fire, and took us home. Once home, in a very caring and concerned manner for his brother Jimmy, my brother Jerry calmly tried to explain how the incident came about…. "Mommy, Jimmy made me do it!"

After all the confessing, crying, spankings, and forgiving, it was back outside for some more fun!

## The raceway down Tank Hill

There was this long winding asphalt road coming down from *Tank Hill*. If we could just build some kind of go cart, it might be fun riding down it. With our dad's help, my brother and I built one using old two-by-fours, plywood, metal rebar, rope for steering, tires we took off our Radio Flyer wagons, plus anything else we could find. It even had a hand-operated wooden brake on a swivel to press against the road to slow it down. Once the wooden swivel brake was finished, I asked my dad, "Are you sure this will stop it?" His response: "No problem, just press the wood against the road once you reach the bottom. It'll do the trick."

So we greased up the wheels and a bunch of us pulled it all the way to the top of the hill. I was the first to try. My brother and the rest of the gang waited at the bottom. Once at the top, it was now ready for the first test run. I strapped myself in and got ready. The kids then gave me a push, and I was off. "Hang on tight, Jimmy." "Okay, let's go!"

## You said the brake would work, dad!

The run was a bit slow at first, but once it reached the steep incline, blue lightning in a bottle cut loose as I barreled down the hill at break-neck speed. The cart then began shaking like a runaway freight train as I held onto the steering ropes with a death grip, my body absorbing the shock of every bump and pothole. After plummeting down the steep grade, I was now getting close to the bottom. "Got to stop this damn thing quick!"

Grabbing the wooden swivel brake stick our dad assured us would work, I pressed it hard against the asphalt road, but the cart wouldn't stop! Wood chips, smoke, sparks, dirt, and dust flying everywhere! Ever try stopping a go cart traveling thirty miles per hour down a steep hill with a piece of wood pressed against an asphalt road? *It doesn't work!*

After crashing and flipping the cart, I end up with a few scrapes, but who cared. "What a rush!" I was now sprawled on the ground expecting my brother and the others to rush over and help me. Instead, he runs over and say's, "How'd the brake work?" "Are you kidding? It disintegrated!" "No problem," Jerry replied. "We'll fix another. Now it's my turn!"

So it was in those days. The raceway down *Tank Hill* became an integral part of our daily adventures. We continued racing the cart down the hill day after day until one of two things happened: either it disinte-grated . . . or we did!

## The grass slide down Tank Hill

There was always plenty of grass on the hillside at *Tank Hill*. Find a big cardboard box, flatten it out, wax up the bottom, sit on it, then hang on for dear life as you careened down the hill. Then back up and do it again. Once the grass flattened out after all the down-hill trips, we could burn rubber all the way! One day my brother Jerry said, "Hey, what about that piece of corrugated metal siding over there?" "Yeah, that might work for a great slide down." So we picked it up, turned it over, then got chased and stung all the way home by a hive of yellow jackets living under it! After a couple hours of recuperating from the stings, it was back up the hill again. Too much fun to be had!

# Chapter 9

# THE "BIG STORE"

## All the basic stuff

Not far from our house was the only housing project store complex. Everyone called it the *Big Store*. It had a food market, barber shop, shoe store, laundry place, TV tube store, a couple of bars, plus a kerosene fuel station nearby. Since our house was heated by kerosene, when Mom sent us kids to the *Big Store* to get something, she would also give us a dime and a container to get some kerosene. Slip the dime into the slot, and out it came.

## Keep your antennas up, Jimmy!

The Big Store was laid out in a rectangle with all the shops configured around its perimeter. It was a new concept in the housing project, and a fun place to visit. Often I would go down alone just to walk around the place and look into the shops. There was this black guy there named Mose who ran his own shoe shine stand outside. He was a nice man, and always said hi to me as I walked by. Each time I visited, I'd stop by to say hi to him. He always greeted me with the same response: "Hey,

Jimmy, what's happening?" "Nothing much, Mose. Just hanging out." "Okay, Jimmy, but keep it straight down here, and keep your antennas up!"

I never really understood what Mose meant when he always told me, "Keep your antennas up." So, one day I asked him, "Mose, what's 'keep your antennas up' mean?" "Jimmy, it means things can get a bit rough down here with some of these punk cat dudes hanging around. Just stay alert." I finally got the picture.

## Is this thing loaded? Let's see!

The *Big Store* also had a large asphalt parking lot behind it. Often, my brother and I would go there to ride our bikes and race around. One day we found this loaded .22-calibre bullet in the lot, and came up with a brilliant idea. We'd get a hammer, lay the bullet down on the asphalt, point it in a direction where there wasn't anything in its path, then hit it as hard as we could with the hammer to see if it exploded! We kept hitting the damn thing over and over, but nothing ever happened. Thank God!

# Chapter 10

## *THE FOOD BUS*

### Yippee! Candy!

There was also this food bus that came around in the housing project every day. It drove up and down the streets, stopping at various spots. The bus had all the basic stuff: milk, eggs, cereals, laundry soap, canned goods, and what we really enjoyed, CANDY! Mom would give us some money and say, "Bring back a quart of milk and a dozen eggs." "Sure, mom, can we buy some candy too?" She always said yes. We'd then run off to catch the bus before it left.

Once inside the bus, it was up and down the aisle getting what mom needed, then the candy! There was this stuff called Red Hots (small little red hearts with a hot bite), and long strings of paper with small candies inside that needed to be pushed out to eat. We also liked Tootsie Pop suckers with hard candy on the outside, and plenty of soft chocolate Tootsie Roll fudge on the inside. They're still made today, but with very little Tootsie Roll Fudge on the inside. But our favorite candies were these small wax candy bottles about two inches long, with different flavored juices inside. They cost about a penny each. Pop 'em in your mouth, then bite on the wax to crack 'em open. The delicious juice then flowed out of the wax bottle, filling your mouth with this fantastic taste. Then spit out the empty wax bottle, and pop in another until all the pennies mom gave us ran out.

## The ice cream vendor

The ice cream cart vendor guy also came around the neighborhood throughout the summer. You always knew he was coming by the music playing on his cart, a Nickelodeon-type tune. "Mommy, can we get an ice cream?" As always, she never said no. We'd then run off with a dime each in our pockets to get our favorite, a thing called an Eskimo Pie.

It was an ice cream bar on a stick covered with chocolate. Had to gulp it down quickly before the chocolate and ice cream melted in the hot summer sun. They're still made today.

# Chapter 11

## *AT THE MOVIES*

## Saturdays at the Rio: Red Top bottle tops got you in

One thing us kids loved to do on Saturday's was go to the movies in downtown Vallejo. There were several movie theaters downtown. But our favorite on Saturday morning was the old Rio theater on Virginia Street.

The Rio was opened in 1947 in a building previously occupied by the Relay Bar. Today, the area where the Rio was located is used as a parking lot.

**Saturday at the movies - mystery serials, cartoons......and more!**

Every week mom ordered bottled milk from the Red Top Dairy in Vallejo. The milk was brought right to our front door by a guy who wore a white uniform, a white hat, and drove up in a Red Top Dairy truck. We called him the *Milk Man*. The dairy had a neat Saturday morning promotional movie program. All you had to do was save up a bunch of cardboard bottle tops that sealed the milk bottles, then take 'em to the movie with ten cents, and that got you in. The Red Top Dairy cardboard tops could only be used at the old *Rio Theater* on Virginia Street. The theater had just one lane down the middle with seats on the right and left. Every Saturday they showed cartoons, mystery serials, cowboy pictures, and science fiction films all day long. Our folks would give us some extra change for popcorn and candy, drop us off around ten in the morning, then come back and pick us up around three o'clock. It was a blast, plus a great way for parents to get rid of their kids for the day. After a day at the movie, we'd come home running around pretending we were some of the characters in the films; cowboys, Indians, cops and robbers, and spacemen.

## The "Claw"

One of the mystery serials shown at the Rio each week was *The Claw*, a sinister evil villain dressed in black who had a long lobster-like claw for a hand. You never saw his face as he spoke in a low raspy voice. He headed up a gang of cutthroats and fifth columnist traitors who secretly supported the Nazi regime in Germany. Every week the black and white episodes showed the Claw's attempt at sabotaging parts of the American Industrial Complex, plus the efforts of the good guys to thwart his plans. Each serial ended in what appeared to be a dramatic failure of the good guys to stop the Claw and his gang from doing damage. "To be continued next week at this theater." You then came back the following week to see if the Claw and his gang prevailed. As it went, the serial picked up where it left off the prior week with the good guys temporarily winning out again.

However, at the end of each serial, the good guys found themselves seemingly losing their efforts over and over against these sinister villains. "To be continued next week at this theater" . . . on and on, for weeks at a time. Couldn't wait to get back to the Rio each week to see if the Claw and his band of cutthroats were finally eradicated from the face of the Earth . . . as long as we had enough bottle tops and a dime to get us in.

## The Durango Kid

My favorite cowboy character was a guy called the Durango Kid, a black-clad wrangler who wore a black mask, rode a white horse, and outwitted rustlers and outlaws every Saturday at the Rio.

## Flash Gordon vs. Ming in outer space

A popular weekly outer space science fiction thriller at the Rio and also on TV in those early days was Flash Gordon. Flash was this space guy played by popular actor Buster Crabbe. He was commissioned by the United States government to travel to the planet Mongo to match wits against its evil ruler Ming, who had Mongo on a collision course to destroy Earth. The serial was produced during the late thirties and released well into the forties.

The Flash Gordon series highlighted all the latest innovative special effects including space ships hung on strings bobbing around in the air floating across the sky, powdered smoke trailing from their exhausts, death rays that looked like Fourth of July sparklers, and many other antiquated creative marvels the special effects guys could muster up in those days. Flash Gordon © King Features Syndicate, Inc.

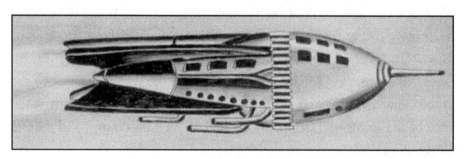

**Flash Gordon Spaceship ~ © Jim Orr ~ Napa Valley Art Studio**

# Chapter 12

# *AT THE ROLLER RINK*

### I won, didn't I?

Roller skating at the local roller rink on Broadway Street in Vallejo was another fun thing to do. We'd jump on our bikes, ride two miles to get there, pay a buck to get in, then rented skates for twenty-five cents. I was eight when I first went.

The first time I went, I learned there was a skating race scheduled for my age group. I couldn't skate worth squat, but why not give it a try. So I signed up, got my skates on, then jumped in line with nine other eager competitors. The starter then said, "Okay, boys and girls, the race is six times around the track. Line up over here and get ready. The winner gets this nice shinny trophy and some free skating tickets." With that, he raised a flag and said, "Get ready, get set, go!" We're off!

I'm now flying around the rink as best I could, staying up with most of the other kids the first couple laps. Then they all started to leave me behind, one by one, but I was still hanging in there. I looked around, and the other nine kids were now bunched up together on the other side of the rink. I'm now alone, skating as fast as I could. I thought, *Hey, man, I'm winning! Wow, I'm way ahead, and there's only one lap to go!* But the others were coming fast behind and starting to catch me. Finally, I crossed the finish line just in time, the rest of the kids breathing down my neck. I began jumping for joy. "Show me the money!" Practically breaking my neck, I make a mad dash up to the man to get my trophy and free skating tickets. But he's standing there giving the trophy and free skating tickets to a girl! After she walked away with all her goodies, I asked the man, "Sir, I thought I won. Does this mean I don't get a nice shiny trophy and some free skating tickets?" "Yes, I'm afraid it does, son. You see . . . you came in last place—an entire lap behind! Have a nice day."

"LAST PLACE?"

# Chapter 13

## *THE GANG NEEDS A FORT*

### The "Hidden Fort" at Mini Ranch

Not far from our house was the Mini Ranch, where they raised cattle and other animals. There were always tons of hay stacks in the main barn, so our gang decided to build a hidden fort inside the haystacks. Hey, when you need a fort, you gotta build it someplace, right? It would take a lot of planning and secrecy, since there were always workers around.

But if the plan worked, we'd have a secret place to hang out. After sneaking into the ranch often to work on it, we finally finished. All we had to do was pull one haystack away to open the front door, go in, then pull it back in to hide us from the world. We stored all kinds of stuff inside for our secret meetings. It was great for a long time, but then one day we went back and found everything in it gone. We forgot one thing. Cows eat a lot of hay!

## On to the next fort up on Tank Hill

Having lost the hidden fort at Mini Ranch, we needed another. Why not build a fort under ground up on *Tank Hill?* Although we considered ourselves "experienced contractors," this job would require some "professional" help! So we asked Eddie, this older black kid in the neighborhood if he could give us a hand. He was a great friend, liked us a lot, and agreed to help. After laying out a plan, we climbed up the hill each day and began digging. Day after day, the digging continued until the underground fort was finally completed. It took forever, but when finished, it was a work of art, a new place for the gang to meet and hang out. Then some cranky resident in the housing project turned us in. They thought it was "too dangerous" for young kids. Give me a break! The Housing Authority workers then came and bulldozed the whole damn thing underground....Tyrants!

## Now we need another fort:
## The "Tree Fort" at Chabot Lake

In the early fifties, Chabot Lake was surrounded by only trees and a small nine-hole golf course. Today, the popular theme park Marine World sits on the property. Down in a deep gulley next to the lake was a grove of eucalyptus trees. Our gang hiked down one time to check it out and found it was very secluded, the perfect place for a fort. It was also right next to the spillway from Chabot Lake with a large pool at the bottom where we could fish.

We cut down some smaller trees and built a tree fort, going there often to hang out, fish, and just do what most of us kids did then: have fun!

# Chapter 14

# *FISHING UP AT MRS. HOLMES' PLACE*

### Our favorite teacher

We've all had at least one. Mine was Mrs. Holmes. She taught our fifth grade class at Everest School in the Chabot Acres housing project. Mrs. Holmes was a sweet, unmarried older woman. She always dressed in simple, conservative Victorian clothes, with her hair pulled up in one of those tight balls in back. She had no children of her own, but loved kids. For some reason she especially liked my best friend Jimmy and me, even though we gave her fits in class all the time.

Like most kids, we couldn't wait for school to end each day. Once the bell rang, Jimmy and I pole-vaulted out the door for some after school fun that usually took the form of either chasing girls, or catching banana spiders in a local ditch. Sometimes we'd run and hide under the wooden walkways at school, looking up between the slats to see under the girls skirts as they walked by. But even that couldn't rival our favorite pastime: *fishing!*

Jimmy and I usually sat next to each other in class, so we talked a lot. Mrs. Holmes scolded us often for this. One time she threatened to separate us if we didn't stop. So we promised to stop talking, but instead began sending secret notes back and forth. We sure weren't sharing about geography or history, always fishing! One day Mrs. Holmes caught me slipping a note to Jimmy. She promptly confiscated it, then asked us both to stay after school. She wanted to talk to us about something. We knew we were in big trouble.

After school, she sat us down in her office as we waited for the cyclone to hit! She then opened my note. Peering down at us with a penetrating, stern look, she said, "Now let's see what this says, boys, shall we?" As we sat petrified, she began reading my note to Jimmy out loud. "Hey, let's grab our poles and book over to Chabot Lake after school to see if they're biting. I've already got the worms at my house." After reading the note, Mrs. Holmes looked down at us again, smiled, and said, "You boys really like fishing, don't you?"

In a reserved and cautious manner, we both responded simultaneously, "Uh . . . yes we do, Mrs. Holmes." She then said something that practically knocked us off our chairs. "How would you like to come up to my place in Napa some Saturday and go fishing? There's a great creek right behind my house with plenty of trout in it." In shock and disbelief, Jimmy and I turned and looked at each other. "Huh?"

Can't say how long it took us to reply to Mrs. Holmes' invitation. We just continued staring at each other in a daze, not saying anything. "Well, boys, would you like to come up, or not?" Still in shock, I finally responded. "Uh . . . yes, Mrs. Holmes. Could we please come up this Saturday?" "Sure, I'll give you directions." "Gee, thanks, Mrs. Holmes!"

## Mrs. Holmes' place up in the Napa Valley

Mrs. Holmes lived in the Napa Valley Wine Country, about thirteen miles away. In those days, the now famous wine region was simply a rural country setting, miles from any place, with only a few scattered wineries. We still couldn't believe what had happened. As ten year olds, how could we ever have comprehended the deep meaning of such an unselfish caring gesture on Mrs. Holmes part? Not until years later did I realize its significance. An act of unconditional love from an old woman who loved kids, had none of her own, and decided to extend that love to a couple of rowdy fifth grade brats who didn't deserve it at all.

In the Bible, Jesus went up on a mountainside and began teaching his disciples. In Matthew 6:19-20 he taught about storing up treasures in heaven. "Do not store up for yourselves treasures on earth, where moth and rust destroy, and where thieves break in and steal. But store up for yourselves treasures in heaven, where moth and rust do not destroy, and where thieves do not break in and steal. For where your treasure is, there your heart will be also."

Mrs. Holmes was obviously a person who believed in God and expressed true Christian principles. I'm confident she had plenty of treasures stored up for her when she walked through those heavenly gates.

## The treasure hunt

Jimmy stayed over at my house that Friday night in April of 1950. Mrs. Holmes had given us a map to her place, so it was kinda like a treasure hunt. We dug up our worms the night before, tied our poles to our bikes, set the alarm for four in the morning, then hit the rack thinking about the next morning's adventure. Watching the alarm clock every half hour was like watching wet paint dry. Never slept a wink. Just talked about the usual stuff: school, girls, and what really mattered . . . fishing! "Hey, its four in the morning! Let's go!" I turned off the useless alarm, jumped out of bed, then got ready for the breakfast Mom said we had to eat before leaving. Breakfast? Forget that! Grabbed a couple of apples, some cheese, our water bottles, then jumped on our bikes waiting out front. Down the road we went, our tires spinning and smoking toward Napa.

In those days, there was only a two-lane road from Vallejo to Napa. One lane up, one lane back, a long thirteen-mile trip. It was a beautiful Van Gogh-like starry sky morning. Whistling down the road with the wind blowing in our faces, we peddled as fast as we could. No special gears on bikes in those days for climbing hills, just sheer leg power. At times, the road would climb to a high peak as we struggled to the top. Once there, it was blue lightning down the other side, a bug or two splattering in our faces now and then as we raced to the bottom.

## Thirteen miles of sweating anticipation

After the long arduous trek, the map finally led us to Lone Oak Avenue, a rural country road. We were to follow it all the way to the end where we'd find an old Victorian house next to a fruit orchard. "This is it, let's go!" Dust flying off our worn out tires, down the road we motored. "There it is, the old house she told us about." As we approached it, we saw Mrs. Holmes outside watering her garden. She saw us coming, and came down the path to greet us with a big hug. "Well, I see you made it boys. Must have been a hard trip. Come on in and have some lemonade."

The inside of the house was like a museum. Old stuff all around, walls covered with some type of silk cloth, antique pictures, huge colorful rugs covering the floor, large wooden stairways and banisters leading upstairs. A really cool place like nothing we had ever seen. Mrs. Holmes then took us into the kitchen and gave us each a glass of ice cold lemonade. "Come on, boys, I'll show you where you can go fishing."

We then walked through the house toward the back door. Once opened, a brilliant yellow carpet of mustard plant and white daisies rolled out across an orchard where a few cows were sleeping. We then heard the sound of trickling water in the background. Jimmy and I looked at each other, bug eyed! "Just follow the path, boys. It will lead you down to the stream. Hope you catch something." We quickly ran back out front, got our poles and can of worms, then scurried through the meadow past sleeping cows and zooming dragon flies. The map had finally led us to the treasure . . . only steps away!

## Morgana King: "It's a lazy afternoon"

Born on June 4, 1930, the American jazz singer and performer Morgana King is best known for her role as Carmela Corleone in the 1972 blockbuster movie *The Godfather*. But she was also a wonderful singer. I remember her best for her song, "It's a Lazy Afternoon." Often, when I experience God's gift of nature and its beauty, certain words in that song come to mind, a reminder of that great day in the spring of 1950 at Mrs. Holmes' house with my best friend Jimmy. The beautiful melody, flutes, and soft flowing violins in the background, then the words. "It's a lazy afternoon, and the beetle bugs are zooming, and the tulip trees are blooming, and there's not another human in view but us two. It's a lazy afternoon, and the farmer leaves his reaping, in the meadow cows are sleeping, and the speckled trout stop leaping up stream. Come spend this lazy afternoon with me."

If the reader is interested in hearing the lyrics of the song, key in this search: "Listen to 'It's A Lazy Afternoon' Song by Morgana King." Then click on the link YouTube dated May 13, 2013. You'll get the picture. Check it out. I promise you'll thank me! Again, make sure its the version published on May 13, 2013 by a guy who put it together for his wife on Mother's Day. Stunning!

## Memories

That lazy afternoon at Mrs. Holmes' house was about to present Jimmy and I with memories we'd carry for a lifetime. As we approached the stream, we could hear the water flowing more distinctly. Finally, there it was, the sun glistening brightly off its surface. Peering intently into the crystal clear water, we saw a number of trout swimming gently back and forth. Suddenly, as we stepped closer, a huge shadow bolted from under the bank, streaking downstream, stopping for only a second, then bolting off again, disappearing in a distant dark pool. "Did you see that?" "Are you kidding? Let's bait up!"

About halfway through the afternoon, Mrs. Holmes came walking toward us through the meadow carrying a tray with something on it. "Hi, boys, catch anything?" "Yep," I replied. Pulling a stringer of trout from the cool water, I gave them to Mrs. Holmes. "Thanks boys, how about some more lemonade, a sandwich, and some cookies?"

## Goodbye old friend

We thanked Mrs. Holmes for a wonderful day, then rode the thirteen miles back home, arriving just after dark. We continued visiting Mrs. Holmes' place throughout that summer, but not long after Jimmy and I parted company, never to see each other again. But if he's still alive, I'm certain he remembers those special days we spent together at Mrs. Holmes' place during the summer of 1950. Interestingly, under completely different circumstances, fifty years later I would visit that same house where Mrs. Holmes once lived.

## Visiting Mrs. Holmes' place fifty years later

As mentioned, Jimmy and I didn't see much of each other after we left the fifth grade. Things just happen that way. New friends, new schools, new experiences, moving to different places. I never visited Mrs. Holmes' house again either, at least not for another fifty years!

At the time I was writing this book, my daughter Kelly and her husband John lived in Napa. Ironically, at one time they just happened to own a house on Lone Oak Avenue, the same street Mrs. Holmes lived on fifty years earlier. One day while visiting them, I drove down the road to see if Mrs. Holmes' house was still there. It was. As I got out of my car, the owner came out and greeted me. We then chatted a while about my experiences there as a young boy. He had heard many great stories about Mrs. Holmes, and allowed me to look around the place. The orchard was still there, but the pristine creek where Jimmy and I had fished fifty years earlier was polluted, and no longer the jewel we had known it to be as kids.

# Chapter 15

# *PIGEONS IN THE PROJECTS . . . AND FROG LEGS*

## Blue Barbs, Trumpeters, Fan Tails . . . Oh my!

Many of us had our own pigeon flocks that flew over the houses each day. We built pigeon coops out of whatever we could scrape up; chicken wire, scrap wood, anything that would work. The pigeons didn't care, as long as they had a place to stay, and food to eat. We all had our own special breed of pigeons, feral rocks, or blue barbs, band tails, trumpeters, and a really cool fan tail if we could afford one. After flying around all day, the flocks returned to their home coups at night to roost.

A fun thing to do was to tie small pieces of paper with secret messages to our pigeons' feet, just like they did in World War I and II. At times, they would land in another kid's coop. If we noticed a stray pigeon in our coop, we'd catch it to see if it had a secret message attached. Often it did.

We also had a special technique to catch any foreigner. Get a wooden box, prop it up with a stick and a long string attached, put a few kernels of corn under it, then wait. Any stray couldn't resist. Once it was under the box, yank the stick, and the intruder was had.

"Wonder who this guy belongs to?" "Hey, isn't that Bobby's fan tail from down the street?" "Yeah, I think so. Looks like a message attached to the foot. Let's check it out."

## Ever eat frog legs?

Although frog legs have nothing to do with pigeons, it was about the same time we had our pigeon flocks that my dad came up with this idea to go frog giggin' to get some frog legs to eat. My brother and I had never heard of it, but my dad heard they were a delicacy to eat, and very expensive in a restaurant. We certainly couldn't afford them, but dad felt he knew a place where we could get some.

Often, as a family we had gone fishing, swimming, and taken picnics up at a place in the Napa Valley called Conn Dam Lake. Dad took a walk once and remembered a large freshwater pond just across the road from Conn Lake that was "bellowing" with bull frogs. But he knew nothing about how to catch them, and they certainly couldn't be caught during the day—just too crafty. They'd jump away before you could even get close. So dad did some research on how to get them, and learned it had to be done at night with a special but inexpensive technique. So the three of us decided to give it a try one hot summer night.

## How we got 'em

We caught them ourselves, and it was fun! The technique was simple. Get a sharp three-pronged frog gig at a local sporting goods store, then hook it on the end of a long bamboo pole. That was your weapon. The next thing needed was a strong high-beam flash light. You were now ready to go, but it took two people to make it work. Upon reaching the pond about nine o'clock one night, we could hear all the bull frogs loud bellowing. Time to go hunting! Simply walk around the pond toward the bellowing sounds using the bright flashlight to locate the bulls. Once spotted, the key was for one of us to keep the light pointed directly in the eyes of froggy, sorta temporarily hypnotizing him, while the other stretched out the frog gig to snatch him. It was tricky, and took a lot of skill and patience. Stretching out that long bamboo pole above the frogs head took skill and agility. Often, froggy would simply catapult himself off the lily pad like a Jupiter Rocket just before one of us launched the gig, but that was where the fun came in. It was you against froggy in a stand off battle of wits and skill! However, at least half the time we hit pay dirt and came home with a load of bulls.

## Time to eat 'em up... good!

Get 'em home, clean 'em up, strip the skin off their legs, then get 'em ready for the next day's meal. Mom would then put flour or corn meal on them, and fry 'em up for dinner. Man, were they good, and not at gourmet restaurant prices! Then, time to plan the next trip up in another week for more!

Oh, and for any of you "animal protection" advocates reading this, one last thing: You may feel our technique for catching froggy bordered on the line of cruel and unusual punishment. That is, driving a razor-sharp three-pronged frog gig through his or her brains (half the time, anyway). Don't worry, bull frogs have never been on the Endangered Species list, and never will be. They love doing basically only five things: eating bugs, urinating, defecating, proliferating . . . and *jumping*!

Gonna get you, froggy!

# Chapter 16

## THE "HIDDEN FOREST"

### A new adventure

Our gang was always going on long hikes, seeking new adventures and places to explore. One time we noticed a span of trees peaking over the top of a high hill, far off in the distance. We decided to hike to it one day to see what was up there. Our moms packed us a lunch the night before, then early before sunrise, we headed off. We finally reached a place where we had to climb over a barbed wire fence, and hike across a long field to reach the base of the hill, but a major problem presented itself. Out of the early mist we noticed a faint sign on the fence: Private Property: Violators Will Be Prosecuted!

We figured that meant if we got caught, they'd probably put us all in prison, or even scarier, maybe the electric chair! So we had to make a quick decision: either go home, or risk it. Still early, the sun was just starting to rise. If we could just get across the field before light, maybe we wouldn't be detected, so we took a vote. "Unanimous—let's go!"

We jumped the fence, and raced across the field undetected. Upon finally reaching the base of the hill, we started climbing. After an hour, we stopped to rest and have a snack.

## Black Widow Spiders!

While resting in a meadow, we noticed large boulders all around us. Always curious, we wondered what might be under them. My buddy Phil turned one over. "Hey, guys, check this out!" Under the rock was a large nest of poisonous black widow spiders. We knew they were black widows from the red hour glass emblem on their stomachs. "Let's catch a few and take 'em home," Bobby said. Phil then got a small jar of peaches from his lunch bag, ate them quickly, cleaned it out, and we all pitched in, carefully catching a few and placing them in the jar. They'd make a great addition to our bug collection back home. Time now to head back up the hill to the summit. The sun was just starting to peak over the crest of the hill, the trees at the top more vivid now, silhouetted against the bright sunlight. Excited and ready for the final assault, we kept climbing. What could be up there?

## Curiosity and adventure: Encourage, or Discourage?

We know God places a sense of curiosity and adventure in kids when they're born. I also believe parents can encourage or discourage this adventurous spirit. I'm grateful my folks didn't restrict my inner desire for adventure. Instead, on most occasions they encouraged me and my brother to venture out to see what might be over the next hill.

## Finally, the top!

Finally reaching the top, none of us spoke a word as we gazed at the beautiful landscape spread out before us. It was the hidden forest we had hoped to find. The trees stretched out forever, closely bunched together. We found an opening, went in, and explored the area for most of the day. Often, we'd see a couple of deer sprinting through the trees, plus all kinds of other animals. After a full day, it was back down the hill, galloping across the field, back to the barbed wired fence and sign that said Private Property: Violators Will Be Prosecuted! After quickly vaulting over the fence, we headed for home with our black widow spiders, and memories of a great day exploring.

Taking care not to be detected, we often returned to that place throughout that summer, known by the secret name we gave it: the Hidden Forest.

## Chapter 17

# *THE COUNTY FAIR*

## Get your latest racing picks—Guaranteed winners!

The Solano County Fair was held each July in Vallejo. The main event was the horse races. Admission was about fifty cents. We could usually scrape up just enough dough to get in, but we needed a lot more for the amusement rides and carnival games along the midway. To get some extra money, we sold racing programs and racing pick forms to those going to the horse races. Each morning, the guy who distributed the forms gave us a bunch to sell.

We got to keep a small percentage of any sales we made. Standing at the gate, we'd repeat the same pitch over and over: "Get your latest racing program and picks here. Guaranteed winners!" "Get your latest racing program and picks here. Guaranteed winners!" After we sold our allotment, we got paid our small percentage, and hit the midway with our newfound wealth!

## Four hours working, fifteen minutes spending!

There were all kinds of games to play along the midway. Remember the stacked bottles you could throw a baseball at to knock 'em off the table? If you were lucky enough to knock all of them off, you'd win a large stuffed animal worth about fifty cents. There was only one problem: The bottles were made of *lead!* We could never knock them all off the table!

Or what about those glass bottles on a table? Throw a ring over one of the bottle necks and win another stuffed animal. Only one minor problem with that as well: The rings had to be dropped directly over the top of the bottles, straight down, to even have a well digger's chance of fitting over the bottle neck. Impossible! But it was a fun way to spend the day.

Four hours in the hot sweltering sun selling racing forms, fifteen minutes spending all the money we earned!

## Chapter 18

# *SPORTS IN THE HOOD AND AT SCHOOL*

### Baseball in the dirt field continues

I really enjoyed playing all kinds of sports with the rest of the gang in the neighborhood and at school. Just as we did when we were younger, we carried on the tradition of playing baseball out in the dirt field below *Tank Hill* behind our house. However, our games were now mostly confined to Saturdays because of school.

### Football on the maintenance lawn

Another thing we did was play football on the local housing authority building lawn, especially after it rained. No pads in those days, just solid hits, and sliding forever on the wet grass and in the mud. It was a blast. Never thought about how the housing authority would react to us messing up their lawn. But they eventually found out, and so did our parents!

## Bay Area "Organized" Baseball

Back in the 50's there were only two pro baseball teams in the Bay Area, both minor league teams: the Oakland Oaks and the San Francisco Seals. I couldn't afford to go to the games, and my dad was never really into sports, or taking me to any of them. But I did have a radio. On hot days I'd take it outside with a blanket, a drink, and some snacks, then set things up. I'd flip on the radio, and be in baseball heaven for the next couple of hours.

## Fun up at the "Rec"

Up from our house in Chabot was a recreation building with a basketball court. We all called it the Rec. It was a great place to spend time playing ping pong, hanging out, or getting together for a pick-up basketball game. I spent practically every night at the Rec.

## New school, new friends - You know the drill

We attended Hogan Junior High until the new school was completed in Chabot Acres. While at Hogan, I was on the basketball teams. See photo's of those teams on next page.

**My best friend Phil, Number 20: A few years before his horrific auto accident**

**City Championship Team, Second in North Bay League; I'm No. 40.**

Wes Matthews, the coach of our city championship team seen in the photo above, was a really cool guy, always respectful and helpful.

He rarely yelled at us, and knew how to bring out our best. He was a real kids coach. Not only did he strive to bring out the best in us athletically, he was equally interested in us as people, and always stressed the importance of education and decent core values in life. This was his highest priority with all of us. He coached and taught for many years in Vallejo. As I grew older and eventually became a Probation Officer in the region, I would often meet with him to help resolve problems he was experiencing with some of his troubled students or athletes.

## Football: Made the team, broke the shoulder

**First Varsity Football Team at Chief Francisco High.**
**Author back row, second from right.**

After three years at Hogan, the construction of Chief Francisco High in the Chabot Housing Project was finally completed, so those of us who lived there headed back out for the tenth grade. Chief Francisco High initially had about two hundred students, with a predominantly black student body. There were about thirty or so of us "white patties," as we were called at the school. The school had just organized its first varsity football team, so I tried out for it. There wasn't all the fancy formations in football back then; pretty basic stuff on offense and defense. No split ends or "wide receivers." The pass catchers were known as "ends"; one on the right side (the right end), the other on the left side (the left end). The defense was also pretty elementary; seven on the line, two linebackers, and two deep backs.

Although my depth perception was a bit off due to partial blindness in my left eye from birth, I could run fast, and decided to try out for right end on offense. I made the team, but my football career didn't last long. The coach also had me playing defense as a linebacker. One day I tackled a runner coming through the line in a scrimmage game. That ended any thoughts of my playing football in the future. I broke my left shoulder and dislocated it at the same time. The injury required an extensive operation, and three months in a body cast, then two more months of physical therapy trying to get my left arm to straighten out.

Because the football injury took so long to rehab, I couldn't play on the basketball team. The coach then asked me if I wouldn't mind being a manager. You know, basically the water boy during the season. I agreed, and joined the basketball team while rehabilitating from the football injury.

**Varsity Basketball Team, Chief Francisco High School, 1956.
Author Jim Orr, back row, second from left without uniform.
Earsell Mackbee, back row, fourth from left, went on to
play pro football for the Minnesota Vikings, participating
in Super Bowl IV against the Kansas City Chiefs.**

In the above photo, my best friend Phil is standing to my left, a year and one half before his horrific auto accident. Phil was an outstanding baseball and basketball player. He helped the teams at Chief Francisco High have terrific seasons during 1956 and 1957. Unfortunately, in the spring of 1958, Phil and a couple other friends were involved in a terrible auto accident that took the lives of one friend, a young baby in another car, and rendered Phil a quadriplegic for life. That story is covered in Chapter 31.

## News articles regarding football injury

FATE - A stuntman piles his car through a solid wall of bricks at 65 miles per hour and lives to tell the story. Walking down the street, the same dare-devil slips on a banana peel and fractures an arm.

A junior high school football player plays in four games without receiving a scratch, but while making a routine tackle in practice he falls on his shoulder and breaks it.

**Vallejo Times Herald - September 22, 1955**

## Football Injury

THE INJURY occurred when Jim Orr, a 15 year old Chief Solano Junior High School end, suffered a broken shoulder in a scrimmage game Tuesday.

Orr, a regular starter for Solano, played four games of rough, tough football for his team without being injured, but became a statistic on an ordinary run-of the mill tackle.

"It was just one of those things," Julian Miguel, Jim's coach at Chief Solano, said as he described the accident. "A runner broke loose into the secondary and Jim had an easy shot at him. Similar tackles are made 20 times a day during scrimmage. We were all surprised to see Jim lying on the ground after the play was over. He's a fine player and a good student; we hated to lose him," Miguel said.

**Vallejo Times Herald - September 22, 1955**

# Football Injury

Taken to Kaiser Foundation Hospital, Jim was placed in traction. Yesterday, he had the broken bone reset. The 145 pound tenth grader is expected to remain in the hospital for five or six days.

His mother, Mrs. James Orr reports that Jim is in fine spirits in spite of his stroke of mis -fortune.

Jim's morale received a lift Wednesday when a group of Solano players paid him a visit at the hospital. Mrs. Orr, who was present at the time said, "It was wonderful of the boys to take time out to visit him."

Mrs. Orr told how Jim constantly talked football when he was at home. "I know he will miss it terribly," she said.

**Vallejo Times Herald - September 22, 1955**

## Football Injury

# Solano Eleven Plays Woodland JV's Today

A small band of Solano Junior High School football players, their ranks including only 22 gridders, will travel to Woodland today for a practice game with the Woodland Junior Varsity at 3:15 PM.

Coach Julian Miguel's Solano eleven possessing a 2-2 record for the season, lost a first stringer for the remainder of the year Tuesday when end Jim Orr suffered a broken shoulder bone.

ORR, A STEADY, hustling performer, received his injury while making a tackle in the open field during a Solano scrimmage.

The chiefs, one of the most surprising teams in the city Junior High league, have been scored upon only twice in four games. Franklin earned one of the TD's and defeated Solano 7-6, while the Vallejo Papooses accounted for the second touchdown last Saturday and edged the Chiefs 7-0.

**Vallejo Times Herald - September 24, 1955**

# Who ripped off my Chuck Taylor tennis shoes?

There was another interesting thing about the football team I played on. This black kid who played left end eventually went on to play professionally in the NFL as a defensive halfback for the Minnesota Vikings. The highlight of his career was playing in Super Bowl IV, where the Vikings lost to the Kansas City Chiefs, twenty-three to seven. However, there was a much less positive thing I remember about this kid during our days in gym class, something that affected me personally.

The best sports tennis shoes in those days were called *Chuck Taylors*. They're still well known today. Chuck Taylor was a famous American basketball player known for his association with the second best-selling shoe in history. It was made by the Converse Shoe Company. Every kid in sports had to have a pair if they could afford them. I saved up enough money, and eventually got some. I wore them everyday in gym class while playing basketball. One day after class, I undressed and showered, leaving my Chuck Taylors on a bench by my locker. *Big mistake!* When I returned, they were gone. I reported the loss to our gym teacher, telling him my name was clearly printed on the shoes.

The next morning in gym class, we all lined up for roll call. In disbelief, I looked down the line and saw this same kid from the football team actually wearing my tennis shoes with my name still on them! Talk about dumb! Our gym teacher promptly dealt with this genius, and returned the shoes to me. The redeeming factor about this story is that as an adult, this star football player became an example to troubled youth in the Minneapolis, Minnesota area, working as a counselor and advisor for local youth outreach and educational programs.

# THE ROCK n' ROLL
# 50's AND 60's

## Chapter 19

## *RHYTHM AND BLUES: JUNIOR HIGH*

### Soul music

As noted earlier, there were about two hundred students at Chief
Francisco High, mostly African American, and only twenty or thirty
of us "white patties." But being white in a majority black school had its
advantages. One was the cool music the black kids listened to, mostly
soul rhythm and blues. As a young teenager I grew up with it, and loved
it! KDIA "Lucky" 1310 was a rhythm and blues radio station out of
Oakland, California. Another, KSAN 1450, was out of San Francisco.
Both blasted out soul music all day long. Couldn't get enough of it!

### The singing groups

There were many great soul music singing groups in those days. One
of my favorites was Little Anthony and the Imperials. I also liked Fats

Domino, Chuck Berry, the Duprees, the Harp-Tones, the Del-Vikings, and the Miracles. The record discs were called 45's or 78's.

They spun on a turntable at either 45 RPM or 78 RPM. No CDs then. The round 45's were seven inches wide, and had a one-inch diameter hole in the middle that slipped over a spindle on your record player. The round 78's were twelve inches wide and had a much smaller hole in the middle. It also slipped over a spindle on the record player. A needle device then dropped down and engaged the disc as it spun on the turntable, then the music came out through a speaker.

One day I heard this new song on the radio by the El Dorados. The song was titled "Crazy Little Mama." I had to have it. Check it out on YouTube. You'll hear a piece of the music we were all into in those days.

## Got to get to the record shop!

I rounded up a couple of bucks and took the ten-cent bus downtown. At the time, there was only one store in Vallejo where you could buy such music. It was a hole-in-the-wall place located down at the end of lower Georgia Street by the pier, just across from Mare Island Naval Shipyard. The owner was this really hip black guy. Once downtown, I got off the bus and started walking down Georgia Street. The lower section had a notorious reputation for its many taverns, pawn shops, gaming parlors, cheap hotels, and all kinds of old buildings with small doors and stairs leading up to who knows where. As I was walking along, suddenly I heard a *BANG!* from directly across the street.

Immediately after I heard the loud bang, I turned, looked across the street, and saw this guy stagger out of a pawn shop doorway and fall flat on the sidewalk. A crowd quickly gathered, and eventually the police and an ambulance arrived. Photographers were now all over the place taking pictures. The ambulance guys picked the guy up off the sidewalk, put him on a stretcher, shoved him inside, then sped off with sirens blaring. It looked like maybe the guy had been shot. After all the commotion ended, I headed back down the street to the record store.

The next day I saw a picture on the front page of the *Vallejo Times Herald* newspaper of a guy lying on a sidewalk on lower Georgia Street. The caption under the photo read "Man shot dead during robbery attempt at pawn shop on lower Georgia Street." The loud bang I'd heard was the pawn shop owner shooting the guy dead! Never a dull moment down on lower Georgia Street.

## Finally got to the record shop

I finally made it to the record shop and got the record *Crazy Little Mama* by the El Dorados. I took it home, played it a few times, then called up my friend Phil. "Hey, Phil, remember that new song by the El Dorados I told you about? I got it!" "Great, bring it over and we'll stick it on the turntable." I booked over to Phil's house, and we began playing the song so loud the walls started vibrating! We were both in a solid groove, clapping our hands to the beat, and dancing around, when suddenly Phils dad bolted into the room!

## You mean you don't like it, Mr. Draper?

After bolting through the door with this shocked look on his face, Phil's dad exclaimed, "What the hell is that? Turn that damn thing off!" I responded, "Gee, Mr. Draper, this is really cool stuff, man. Don't you like it?" His response: "Are you crazy?!"

If Mr. Draper was around today, I guess his reaction would be the same, or probably worse regarding the type of music young folks are subjected to these days. Frankly, I wouldn't blame him. Much of the music young folks listen to today is laced with violence, political agendas, loud clanging noise, and rap-laden lyrics you can't even understand. That wasn't the case during the *Rock n' Roll 50's and 60's.* At least you could comprehend what the groups were singing about. The counterfeit, hard-edged, delusional crap called "music" today is nothing more than a bunch of obscure gibberish that hurts your ears and numbs your senses. More importantly, a lot of it glorifies and even encourages violence and criminal behavior. No thanks, not the type of fake music I would allow my kids to listen to.

## Chapter 20

# *FAVORITE SINGERS, DANCES, AND DJ'S*

---

### The Blues

I can't list them all, but here's a few I liked. You can check them all out on *You Tube*.

#### *John Lee Hooker*

Blues singer John Lee Hooker was one of my favorites. Most white kids in those days never heard of him. But he stood out in the housing project where I grew up. Listen to one of his most popular songs, "Boom, Boom, Boom, Boom" on YouTube.

#### *Jimmy Reed*

Jimmy Reed was another favorite. The song that stood out for me was "Bright Lights, Big City."

# Rock n' Roll

## *Fats Domino*

Everyone loved Fats Domino. Fats was one of the pioneers of *Rock n' Roll* music. He never sang a bad song. Many of us would have certain songs of the day embroidered on the back of our jackets. I liked Fats Domino's song "I'm Walkin'," so I had it embroidered on the back of mine. But the Fats Domino song I liked the most was "The Fat Man."

## *Chuck Berry*

Before Elvis, Chuck Berry was the real "king" of *Rock n' Roll.* All his songs were great. After school, some of us would go down to the "corral," a cafe a short distance from Vallejo High to hang out, play the juke box, and dance. Kids all across America did the same, heading to their favorite juke joints after school. In 1957, Chuck Berry did a song about this experience called "School Days." Another was "Johnnie Be Good." Listen to them both on *YouTube.*

Lee Andrews and the Hearts, "Teardrops"

The Marcels, "Blue Moon" (1961)

The Chiffons, "He's So Fine"

The Marvelettes, "Please, Mr. Postman" (1961)

Later on in the sixties, the Beach Boys from Southern California came along, and went straight to the top. Here's a couple of their hits. Simply go to *You Tube* to listen to these songs: "Good Vibrations" and "I Get Around."

## Dances

There were many popular dance steps during the 50's that complemented the songs of the day. One of the most popular was the *Twist*, which emerged from a song called "The Twist" by singer Chubby Checker. A few others included the Stroll, Bop, Bunny Hop, and Mashed Potato. Many of the new dances were featured on the popular afternoon TV program *American Bandstand* out of Philadelphia, hosted by Dick Clark. Kids across America watched the program every afternoon where they could view other teens doing all the latest dance steps to songs played by station DJ's, or performed live on stage by the actual artist or singing group.

## The "DJ's" - Wolfman Jack

During the 50's and 60's there were many great Disc Jockey's or "DJ's" who played *Rhythm & Blues* and *Rock n' Roll* music on the radio. During the 60's, one of the most well known was a guy named Wolfman Jack. With his trade mark "howl" and distinctive "gravelly" voice, he lit up the airways with what many considered subversive sounds of black *Rhythm & Blues* music that had been banned from "Mainstream" AM Radio.

Born Robert Smith in Brooklyn, New York, the Wolfman attended Virginia's National Academy of Broadcasting and eventually ended up in Mexico working for the powerful XERB-AM radio station in 1965. It was there he became a radio legend. At the height of his popularity, his "mysterious" identity was still unknown. At that time, the Wolfman was having a major influence on *Rhythm & Blues* music as it found its way into mainstream radio. The "mystery" of Wolfman Jack was finally solved when he appeared in the popular movie American Graffiti in 1973. The Wolfman died on July 1, 1995 at the age of 57.

# Chapter 21

# GROWING UP IN THE 50'S
# AS A TEENAGER

## Innocence and *Rock n' Roll*

Growing up in Vallejo as a teenager in the late 50's was a blast. It was a time of innocence, Rock n' Roll, Motown music, car clubs, cruisn' in your rod on Friday and Saturday nights, drive-in movies, plus tons of other things that made the 50's unique in American history. You were either there, or wish you were. Sure, there were problems, especially during the post-World War ll "Atomic Bomb" era. The Russians are coming! There were air raid drills at school, plus practicing getting under our desks constantly, as if a desk would help in a real air raid.

We all felt *"The Bomb"* could blow up over our heads at any time, especially since we lived near Travis Air Force Military Base, only a few miles away in Fairfield, California, a definite target in the Russian crosshairs. Often a large B-36 bomber from the base would come rumbling across the sky over Vallejo, its six massive prop engines blowing out a loud vibrating noise you could hear miles away. They carried *A-bombs* and were called "lumbering cows." Each B-36 could take off from a base on this continent, penetrate enemy defenses, destroy any major industrial area in the world, then return non-stop to the point of take-off. Sure, we were scared at times about all this, but in the big picture it didn't matter. Too much fun to be had! Too many things to do! No wasting time on video games, computers, or hand held devices demanding our attention then. But one thing we did do a lot was talk on our home phones to our buddies, girlfriends, or boyfriends. When I overdid it on our phone, my mom would often say, "Five more minutes, Jimmy, and that's it! And get off the phone if our neighbor Mabel comes on the party line and wants to use it!"..............party line?

## Party line phones - We all had them

During those early days, we had "party line phones," and I don't mean like "having a party." They were called "party lines" because you actually had to share a phone line with a few other families in the neighborhood. At any given time, you might pick up your phone and hear the other "party" talking on it. You could also speak directly to them as well! "Oops, sorry, Mabel. How long will you be on the phone?" "Only a few more minutes, Jimmy."

On the other hand, you could be on the phone talking to someone and another person on your party line might interrupt to use the phone. With smart phones, computers, and all the modern technology we have today, talking about a shared phone line probably seems unreal. But it was all we had in the early days of the 50's, and it worked just fine.

# Chapter 22

# PLUTO'S, PING PONG, HARD TOPS, CRUISN'

## Pluto's and Ping Pong

While at Vallejo High, there was one thing a couple of us enjoyed practically every lunchtime. First, we'd grab a quick hot dog at Pluto's down the street, the best hot dog in town. Then, it was time for a serious game of ping pong with a couple of adults who owned businesses along Tennessee Street. One of them owned a clothing store, the other a delicatessen. In the back of the deli was a room with a regulation ping pong table. Can't remember how we ever got hooked up with these guys, but they enjoyed having us compete with them. My friend Phil and I were pretty good at the game and battled out some serious doubles games with these older dudes every lunchtime.

## "Hard Top" auto races behind Chabot housing project

Out behind the housing project in Chabot was this circular dirt racing strip. Every Friday night during the summer the hard-top auto races were held there. The hard tops were nothing more than a forties-type car model modified for racing. It was a fun way to spend a Friday night with our buddies and girlfriends. My girlfriend Ruth's dad owned a hard top, and raced it every Friday night.

## Cruisn' in Town

Cruisn' up Georgia Street in the '55 Chevy.
Mare Island Naval Shipyard in far background across the straits below lower Georgia Street. Notice all the "erector set" type TV antennas on the roofs used in those days for TV reception.

# Chapter 23

# *SNEAK'N IN THE MOVIES*

## Saturdays at the "Flicks" - Never enough dough to get in!

As teenagers, we tried to go to the movies a lot on Saturdays, but never had enough money for all of us to get in. So we had to come up with a plan. We called the movies the "flicks." "Hey, let's all go to the flicks this Saturday." Slang for "film," the term *flicks* was first coined in 1926 due to the "flickering" appearance of the normal rudimentary film used then.

**The Hanlon Movie Theater on Virginia Street in Vallejo, Circa 1950's**

There were several theaters in Vallejo at the time. The El Rey on Tennessee Street, the Strand downtown on Georgia Street, the Rio and Hanlon over on Virginia Street, the Rita out on Solano Avenue, and the Marvel (can't remember where it was). There were also two drive-in movies, the Crescent out behind the Chabot housing project, and the Vallejo Auto Movies in east Vallejo.

## Not enough coins for all of us to get in: How do we do it?

We came up with this plan, and the best place for it to work was at the El Rey down on Tennessee Street. There was this alley outside with an emergency exit leading from inside the theater to the alley. We'd first pool what money we had for two guys and their girls to get in. It was always darkest when the movie first began, so once it started, the guys inside would run to the emergency exit and open it quickly. Waiting outside, once the door flew open, we'd all run in and scatter all over the theater. Someone would always report us to the manager, then the ushers would begin scanning the dark theater with their flashlights looking for us. Some of us got caught and were escorted out. But a few of us were lucky enough to go undetected, and enjoyed the rest of the double feature, unless of course we were making out ( kissing) with our girlfriends during most of the movie.

## Sneak'n in the Drive-In Movies

We used a similar plan to get into the drive-in movies. We'd all chip in the dough for a couple kids to get in who had cars, then the rest of us would hide in the trunk of their cars before entering the drive-in. If the plan worked, once inside and parked, the drivers would let us out of the trunks, then we'd quickly jump in the cars. It was always dark at the drive-in movie, so we rarely got caught. Hey, when you're desperate and don't have the dinero, you've got to come up with some kinda plan, right?

## Favorite movies during the 50's

Everyone has a favorite movie or two that stands out in their minds. During the 50's, three stand out for me. They eventually became classics, and are shown on TV now and then. The Blob was a film starring the famous actor Steve McQueen in his feature film debut. The movie is about a growing, corrosive, alien amoeba-like creature that crashes to Earth from outer space inside a meteorite. It devours and dissolves citizens in the small community of Phoenixville, Pennsylvania. Ironically, in 1966 while in the army, my wife Joan and I were both stationed at Valley Forge General Hospital, which just happens to be in Phoenixville. Small world! Fortunately, we weren't there when those in the town were "dissolved" by The Blob!

The Blob grew larger, redder, and more aggressive, eventually becoming bigger than a building. In the movie, it was finally controlled by freezing it, and then was transported to the North Pole, where it remains frozen to this day! On a much sadder note, the movie also reminded me of a more realistic tragic event that occurred in May of 2018. Devastating lava flows were creeping up from cracks all over the big island of Kilauea in the Hawaiian Islands, destroying homes, roads, and threatening a geothermal power plant. At the time, it seemed like a modern day version of The Blob, but this time the Lava Blob!

Rebel Without a Cause was another classic released in 1955 about emotionally confused middle-class teenagers. The film starred James Dean, an up-and-coming iconic actor who lost his life soon after in a car accident. The movie was a groundbreaking attempt to portray the moral decay of American youth, critique parental styles at the time, and explore the gaps between generations. James Dean drove a really cool black '49 Mercury during the movie, a car a couple of my friends also had during the 50's.

Many cool songs were written about the Mercury. "Mercury Blues" was one of the best. Listen to two renditions on the Internet, one by black blues singer KC Douglas, the other by country music star Alan Jackson. They're only a few minutes long each. I think you'll thoroughly enjoy both of them. Check them out on You Tube.

Blackboard Jungle, another classic released in 1955 is a film about teachers trying to make a difference in a violent interracial inner city school. The film is remembered for its use of *Rock n'Roll* music in the soundtrack. In search of the kind of music teens were listening to, director Richard Brooks borrowed a few records from star Glenn Ford's son Peter. When he heard Bill Haley and the Comets perform the song "Rock Around the Clock," he found the perfect theme song, the first rock song ever used in a Hollywood feature. Teens flocked to the film, dancing in theater aisles as the song played over the opening credits. Thanks to Blackboard Jungle, the song hit number one on the billboard charts, eventually selling twenty-five million copies and becoming the National Anthem of *Rock n' Roll.*

# Chapter 24

# *BEING "COOL" IN THE 50'S*

## Looking "Cool"

As a teenager during the late 50's, my friends and I were always trying to be *cool*; look cool, walk cool, dress cool, talk cool, just be as cool as you could. I'm sure it was the same all over the country with teenagers. For us, to act cool you had to walk a certain way, talk a certain way, sit in your car a certain way, do everything a certain way. Walking a certain way meant kinda bobbing your head up and down, with maybe both hands in your pockets as you sauntered along. If you passed someone while either walking or driving in your car, you didn't wave frantically. Instead, it was a slight nod of the head up and down, as if to say, "Hey, what's happening man?"

Another way of looking cool was to style your hair a certain way. The guys "in the groove" combed their hair in what was called a Duck Tail, or Duck Ass style. The first thing was to use this greasy stuff in a can called Dixie Peach that was thick and shiny. As you combed it in, gobs of the stuff seeped through the teeth of your comb. Then you just wiped it off, slapped it back on, and kept combing. Once you were all lathered up, you'd comb your hair in the back with a vertical part exactly in the middle. Then, for the final touch, at the very front of your hair just above your forehead you'd sculpture a Duck Tail-type hook pointing down toward your forehead. You were now greased up and ready for action!

## The "Flat Top"

A lot of the guys would also get their hair cut in a more conservative style called a Flat Top. It was simply a style where the top was buzzed down, leaving about a half inch or so sticking up with the sides left long. The girls, on the other hand, had hairstyles with names such as Bouffant, Page Boy, the Poodle, and a large balloon-type style we guys called the Bird's Nest. My African American friends also had really unique hair styles. Back in those days, a guy named George Johnson in Chicago invented some hair style products most black guys and girls used. The girls used this stuff called Ultra Sheen. The guys used either Ultra Wave or Afro Sheen. Just like Dixie Peach, these products made the guys and girls hair look shiny, slick, and great! But that wasn't all. You also needed to dress cool!

## Dressing "Cool"

"Dressing cool" meant wearing certain clothes. Vallejo had some great stores for shopping. The right clothes and shoes were important to our gang. After saving up, it was time to head downtown for some serious shopping. In those days, we visited Crowley's Department Store, Karl's Shoes, Leed's Shoes, and Florsheim Shoes (my favorite shoe store). The girls liked going to some of the same places, but would rather shop at the upscale City of Paris Department Store on the corner of Georgia and Marin Streets if they could afford it.

**City of Paris Department Store, Corner of Georgia and Marin Streets**

Many of the guys wore Levi's with the cuffs rolled up at the bottom in a very thin roll. Some guys even wore their Levi's very low on the butt, kinda like some dudes wear 'em today, although I never preferred that look.

Most of the guys I ran with also wore their shirt collars turned up in back. I especially liked wearing a brand of shirt called Sir Guy that could only be found at the Sir Guy shirt store on Georgia Street. In the 50's, Sir Guy shirts were popular with many of my Low Rider friends. Wearing a Sir Guy shirt meant you were really cool. They were made with a bright reflective glitter material. With a Sir Guy shirt on at night downtown walking around the city lights, you stood out like a searchlight, practically blinding anyone walking by. I believe they're still made today. Another thing a lot of the guys wore were leather jackets and dark glasses. Pendleton brand shirts were also very popular, but really expensive.

## Talking "Cool"

There was also a unique language we used to communicate with each other in those days, our own independent way of inventing words and phrases to describe things. Many are long forgotten, others still used today. Here's a list of some that were part of our every day lives:

"Baby" (Cute girl ); "bad" (meant "good"; "Man, Larry's car is really looking bad tonight."); "bash" (great party ); "big daddy" (an older person); "blast" (having a good time); "boss" (really great!); "burn rubber" (accelerate fast with your car, laying down a tire imprint on the street); "cool cat" (a really "hip" or in-the-know person); "crazy" (like "crazy man" - a good thing); "cruisn'" (driving around in your car); "cut out" (to leave the scene or premises); "Daddy-O" (to address someone, as in, "Hey, what's happening, Daddy-O?"); "dibs" (a claim to something; "Hey, man, I got dibs on the shotgun [passenger seat] when we go cruisin' tonight."); "dig" (to understand something; "Hey, man, dig that chick, pretty cool huh?"); "floor it" (cram the accelerator in the car to the floor and burn rubber); "going steady" (having a permanent girlfriend or boyfriend; the girl always wore the guys ring on a chain around her neck); "hep," or "hip" (being in the know; "She's really hip."); "making out" (kissing); "pad" (your home); "put down" (saying bad things about someone ); "rod" (your hot car); "slip me some skin" (Rubbing the palm of your hand against another's), "sounds" (music; "That's some cool sounds playing on your radio."); "square" (someone you thought wasn't "cool"); "My Eye!" (term used for exclaiming disbelief); "Get out of town" (exclamation; "Are you kidding me? Get out of town!"); "cat" ("Man, he's a cool cat.")

# Chapter 25

# *FINALLY, MY DRIVER'S LICENSE!*

## Learning to drive at sixteen

As with all teenagers, I couldn't wait for my sixteenth birthday to get my driver's license. I thought it was going to be simple, right? First thing was to learn to drive, then pass the DMV written and driving tests, then off I would go. Not so as simple as I thought. Found that out the hard way!

In the 50's, many cars had three gears to move the car forward; first gear, second gear, and third gear. There was also a neutral gear allowing the car to idle, and a reverse gear to move the car backwards. You had to shift or manipulate the transmission into each gear using a hand held device called a stick shift. It was either on the floor, or next to the steering wheel.

There was also a device on the floor next to the brake called the clutch. Once the car was placed in idle, the trick was to shove in the clutch with your left foot, put the car in first gear with the stick shift lever, then gently let pressure off the clutch with your left foot while pressing down on the gas peddle with your right foot. Pretty tricky. It all took a fair amount of coordination, but if done correctly, the car would move forward without stalling. You'd then repeat the process shifting

---

into second and third gears bringing the car up to speed. It all had to be coordinated in order to work. Otherwise, if you let the clutch out too fast, the car would lurch forward and stall. Not an easy task when first learning to drive. Took a lot of practice with my dad helping. But eventually it became second nature. Once mastered, I was ready for my first drivers test down at the Vallejo DMV. I'll never forget it!

But first, a quick story about my mom's driving habits - or lack thereof! This has nothing to do with getting my driver's license, just thought I'd throw it in here for a laugh.

## Mom never learned to drive—or did she?

For some reason, my mom's nickname was Boots. All my life, that's what people called her, Boots. She never learned to drive, *but thought she could!* While driving around with my mom and dad, I'll never forget her skillful attempts at trying to stop the car as we approached a stop light, even though the light was still two and a half football fields in front of us! Without warning, she would yell out at my dad, "Jim, there's a red light up there! Get ready to stop! Get ready to stop!" With that, she'd launch this highly technical maneuver of "slamming" her "boots" against the front floorboard over and over as she tried to stop the car. But it never worked! "Mom, there's no brake on that side of the floorboard. It's over here on the driver's side!".... "Shut up!"

## My first driver's test at the DMV - Not so good!

I couldn't wait to get to the DMV that Monday morning for my appointment. I had studied hard, knew how to drive like a champ, and was ready to ace the test and get motoring down the road. My dad dropped me off and wished me luck. "I'll pick you up in about an hour, Jimmy. Once you pass, they'll give you a temporary driver's permit. I'll let you drive us home then, okay?" "Sounds great, dad!"

As I ran through the front door of the DMV office, reality suddenly hit me in the face. All the confidence I had before entering melted like a toasted cheese sandwich once inside! I slowly walked up to the counter and introduced myself. A lady with a lit cigarette hanging out of the corner of her mouth then gave me the written drivers test. "Take it over to that counter, sonny. When finished, bring it back. If you pass, you can take the driving test."

Once finished, I returned the test to the lady, who began grading it. After what seemed like an eternity, she called me up to the desk. "You did great, sonny. Now have a seat over there. Your driving instructor will be out shortly." I was now thinking, *Great, I'm halfway there. All I need to do now is pass the driving test!* No problem, right?.... *WRONG!*

## "I'm Mr. Cosmo Schlapp. Get up and come with me now!"

While waiting for the driving instructor, I was thinking, *Don't forget the hand signals for left and right turns. Make sure to look right and left before turning. Watch your speed. Keep your eyes on the road. Don't forget how to parallel park. Watch out for pedestrians.*

Suddenly, the door to my left bursts open, and this three-hundred-pound, six-feet-five behemoth bolts through it. He lumbers across the room, walks straight up to me, looks down, and say's, "Are you Jimmy Orr?" "Uh . . . yes, sir. I am." "My name is Mr. Cosmo Schlapp. I'm your driving instructor. Get up and come with me!"

Ever felt like you were about to be wheeled into the operating room for brain surgery....to be performed by a gorilla?

Mr. Schlapp didn't remind me of the kind, mild, meek-mannered instructor I thought I was expecting. We both then went outside, and he gave me the keys to the DMV car. After a few simple instructions, he said, "Okay, get in and start it up. We'll take that exit over there." He then got in on the passenger side as the car began tilting to starboard. "Start it up. Let's go." Scared stiff, but still confident, I began driving toward the exit next to the DMV building. The "Schlapp" man then said, "Slow down sonny, you're going too fast!"

## Hey! Where'd that pedestrian come from?

All of a sudden this guy walks right in front of me from around the corner of the building. I hit the brakes as the car skids to a stop just before almost *plowing into him!* Mr. Schlapp then peers over at me, and in a kind, encouraging voice exclaims, "What the hell are you doing? Are you kidding me?! Driving test over, sonny. Pull back into the parking lot!"

Devastated, I'm not even out of the DMV lot and almost run over a guy! Once back in the lot, Mr. Schlapp got out and shared a few final soothing words with me. "Well, sonny, you didn't run over the guy, but you did manage to accomplish one major milestone. You now own the record for the shortest driving test in the history of the Vallejo, California DMV! The previous record was two minutes. You did it in under one! Come back in two weeks and try again. Have a nice day."

After brooding over the experience for the next couple of weeks, I finally got a second chance for another driving test, hoping and praying I wouldn't get the "Schlapp Man" again. I didn't. This time I made a resolved effort to not run over anybody, passed, and was in hog heaven, but now I needed a car. I wonder if my dad would let me drive that cool '55 Chevy Bel Aire he just bought?

## Chapter 26

# *POP'S COOL '55 CHEVY*

**1955 Bel Air Four-Door Chevy: The exact style, color, and model of Dad's new car**

## "Can I use it, dad?"

One day my dad came home with this really cool blue and white '55 Chevy Bel Aire he just bought. I asked him if I could ever use it. Never thought he'd say yes, but he did. So one Friday night I picked up my girl Ruth and we headed down to Patches Drive-In for a hamburger, coke, and fries, all for under a buck! After some hangout time with our friends, we cruised around town then headed out to park at this secluded spot we knew. We turned on the radio and began sharing old war stories. A short time later, a police officer came by, ordered us to leave, then drove off. I turned on the ignition to start the car but it wouldn't start. The radio was left on too long, causing the battery to die. My dad instructed me to be home at a certain time and that time was fast approaching. "Now what?" With the battery dead, I needed help fast. Ruth then said, "Hey, Jim, there's a car over there. Maybe they can help." "Yeah, maybe they can help me jump start the car." So I walked over and asked the driver if he could help. In a slurred voice, he responded, "Uh . . . sure, man, I'll help ya." I ran back to the Chevy and opened the trunk, but there were no battery jump cables. I then went back to the same guy and asked if he had any. His response: "Uh . . . we ain't got none." "Can you give me a push then?" "Sure, man, no problem."

## Gettin' ready for the push!

The guy and his friends had obviously been drinking, but I had no choice. I needed their help. I figured I could simply pop the clutch as the car began rolling and start it up. It was an easy procedure in those days to start a car with a dead battery. So I ran back, jumped in the Chevy and got ready for the push. As the headlights of the guys car approached closer and closer from behind, Ruth exclaimed, "Jim, he's coming too fast!" Suddenly, a crash as the Chevy bolted forward. The guy not only gave us a push, he hit us so hard it launched the Chevy forward leaving a large dent in the rear bumper.

## A lot of explaining to do

We did get the car started, but I had a lot of explaining to do when my dad saw the damage. One more thing: I only got to sit in the driver's seat of that Chevy once again!

# Chapter 27

## *GOTTA GET A CAR*

### But where do I get the dough?

As mentioned, I only got to use my dad's '55 Chevy once after the rear bumper incident, so I had to find work to make some money for a car. Finding a job as a teenager during the summer of 1956 was tough, but I did manage to nail down a couple. There was an employment office in Vallejo where you could go and sign up for jobs that came available.

I'd go there each day, sign up, sit down, then wait for my name to be called if a job came up. Got one picking apricots on a farm, then worked on another farm bailing hay. The work was hard under the hot summer sun, but I saved what I could until the next job came along. I also worked on a chicken ranch for a short time. Man, was that messy!

On another occasion, a friend of mine, Dave, called me. "Jim, I got this job selling encyclopedias. The guy needs another person for our neighborhood. Would you like the job?" The chicken ranch job had just ended, so I said, "Sure, Dave, what do I do?" "The guy will train you. You just go door to door explaining what they are, then ask people to buy them. It's easy and you get a percentage of what you sell - simple." Well, it wasn't that simple! I maybe sold one set the whole time I did it. On the other hand, Dave was great at it. He went on years later to become a teacher, then eventually principal of a high school up in Napa. Maybe somehow selling encyclopedias helped set the foundation for his success as an educator? It certainly didn't work out for me. But then another job came along I really enjoyed, one I had already developed a special talent for over the years.

## Painting by the numbers

From the time I was a young, I enjoyed drawing. When I was six, my folks bought me a Paint by Numbers kit. It was the first painting I ever did. Not long ago, my daughter Kelly found it in her grandmother's basement. I still have it today. It was a picture of a fish under the sea. All you did was simply fill in the numbers with the designated paint colors.

Although I was born partially blind in my left eye, I still managed to do a pretty good job of it. From that point on, I became interested in art and pursued it as a hobby. I even originally majored in art at college, but it required too much time and I needed to switch my major, eventually receiving a degree in Health Science. But I always kept my hand in it, exhibiting at art galleries and employing my art skills over time as an avocation.

As mentioned above, in 1956 I was working various jobs doing anything in an attempt to get money to buy a car. Then a job came along that was right in my wheelhouse, one I could apply my art skills to. It was perfect for me during that summer of 1956.

# The Air Force B-52: America's champion nuclear bomber

My dad was working as a machinist at Kaiser Industries in Richmond, California, at the time. The plant manufactured parts for the landing gear of the Air Force B-52 Nuclear Bomber. Apparently some significant mistakes were occurring on certain parts on a regular basis. Some engineer came up with an idea that might help alleviate the problem. If the machinists working on the project had an actual drawing of the part in question, highlighting the spot where the mistakes were occurring, it would be a reminder to "Be careful at this juncture. This is where the error is occurring!" My dad told his supervisor I was pretty good at drawing anything I could look at, so an appointment was set for me to meet with this engineer at the Kaiser Plant to discuss his idea.

On a Monday morning I accompanied my dad to the Kaiser Plant. Once there, I was escorted into a room to wait for the engineer to interview me. After a short period, he came in, introduced himself, and asked me several questions. He then explained his idea about reducing errors on specific parts of the B-52 bomber's landing gear. After this, he left and eventually returned with a large aluminum part, setting it on the floor in front of me. The part had an X marked on it where the tooling error was occurring. He gave me some paper and a drawing kit, and said, "Okay, Jim, draw that part just as it sits there, noting the exact spot on the drawing where the tooling error has occurred. I'll be back in a couple of hours to look at it."

He eventually returned, looked at the drawing, and said, "Not bad, Jim, not bad at all. I think we can use you on this project."

I was hired, and continued to produce drawings of various B-52 Bomber parts throughout that summer until the job finally ended. The drawings resulted in a significant decline in mistakes made by machinists working on them. I really loved that job. With the money I saved during that summer, I was able to get my first car, a 1951 Ford two-door hard top, with a flathead V-8 engine. Couldn't wait to start customizing it.

# Chapter 28

## *GOT THE FORD!*

### Now to customize it

After I bought the '51 Ford, the first thing I needed to do was all the custom body work, which took a long time. I replaced the grill with a Pontiac grill, did more body work and sanding, then prepared it for a new paint job down at P&L Body Shop, a place many of the guys had their cars painted. Painting a car was expensive, so to save money most of us did the preliminary prep work ourselves; sanding off old paint, taping everything that wasn't to be painted, stuff like that. Once the prep work was done, I beelined down to P&L. Upon arriving, the owner Dave said, "Still going with that metal flake rust color Jim?" "Yep." "Okay, we'll have it done for you in a couple days."

Waiting for the Ford to be painted was like getting ready to go fishing. Never could sleep much the night before a fishing trip. After two days of little sleep, I called P&L. "Paint job ready yet, Dave?" "Not yet, Jim. We had some priority body work come in. Haven't started yet. I'll call you when it's ready." "Okay, Dave, I'll wait to hear from you."

Three days later, I got the call. "The Ford's ready, Jim. Come and get it." Couldn't wait to call my best friend Phil. "Hey, Phil, the Ford's done and ready to be picked up. Can you drive me down to P&L?" "Sure, let's go check it out."

Upon arriving, we both walked in and gazed at what to me looked like the Hope Diamond! "Wow, it looks great, Dave!" I then paid for the job, got in, revved it up, and got ready to burn rubber. As I was leaving, Dave said, "Looks pretty cool, Jim. Don't scratch it!" In an instant, I'd become an idol worshipper! "See you down at Patches Drive-In, Phil. Let's bug out."

I was now driving down the road in what I thought was the coolest car in Vallejo. While motoring up Georgia Street, every now and then I caught a glimpse of someone checking it out as I drove by. But now I needed to do a few more things to give it that final "cool" look. First, because of my artistic skills, I added some fancy pin striping to the body, then eventually some cool Appleton spot lights. Finally, there was one more appointment to make down at P&L to get the Ford lowered to street level.

## "Lowering" the Ford

Back in the late 50's and early 60's, the one thing most of us did to our cars was lower them so the entire chassis sat low to the street. It was an extremely expensive process to achieve if you wanted to maintain good suspension and a smooth ride. But who had the money for that? However, there was a less expensive way to do it. Most cars had metal coiled springs about twelve inches long, located by each wheel. They compressed and expanded as the car moved along, absorbing shock and providing a smoother ride. However, if you wanted to lower your car cheaply, you would simply take it down to P&L Body Shop and have Dave put a blow torch to the coil springs! The springs then got white hot. As the springs heated, the weight of the car compressed them flat as a pancake, causing the entire vehicle to sink down. In twenty minutes, your ride was lowered for only about twenty-five bucks. But the cheap lowering job came at a price. The suspension and coil springs were now gone, resulting in the loss of any smooth shock-absorbing ride. Your car now felt like riding around in a Sherman Tank! But you had that cool look for sure, even though your body and those with you in the car absorbed the shock and trauma of every bump and pothole in the road! But who cared. Looking cool was really what mattered. Now that the Ford was customized, it was time to make application to the "Slicks," Vallejo's hottest and most popular custom car club.

## The "Slicks" : Vallejo's coolest car club

The coolest car club in Vallejo at the time was the Slicks, a name derived from a special drag racing car tire. The tires were called Slicks because they had no tread, providing better traction for racing. To belong to this exclusive club, you first had to be sponsored by one of its members, then voted on. I was sponsored, but my application was rejected the first time around. Maybe they thought I was too young. However,

I eventually got accepted and became the clubs youngest member. We all had club jackets called Car Coats with the name Slicks on the back. We also had metal Slicks placards mounted inside the rear window of our cars. With some of the coolest classic cars in Vallejo at the time, we cruised around town in style, and everyone knew who we were.

# Chapter 29

# *CRUISN' ON FRIDAY & SATURDAY NIGHTS*

## Pick up your girl, then meet the gang at the Drive-In Restaurant

Across America during the *Rock n' Roll'n* 50's and 60's, the same *American Graffiti* scene played out on weekends. For us, we'd pick up our girls and head down to Patches or Eat n' Run Drive-Ins to meet the rest of our buddies and their girls. After grabbing a burger, coke, and fries, we'd hang out yakking, or checking out all the latest custom work done on some of the cars. There was always someone who had just done some "upgrading" on their engine plant. They may have added duel carburetors or a new camshaft for higher engine performance, or duel mufflers for that really cool rumbling sound. Then there was always the guy who had just returned from Tijuana, Mexico where he added new popular "tuck and roll" leather upholstery to his rod. Tuck and roll was very expensive up here in the states, but in Mexico you could have it done in a couple of days at a fraction of the price.

So, in essence, meeting at Patches or Eat n' Run Drive-Ins was like going to a mini "Show n' Shine" Classic Car Show. Then, after all the yakking and hang'n out, it was time to get ready for the evening cruise downtown.

**Hang'n out at Patches Drive-In Restaurant before a Friday night cruise**
**Dudes to left standing in front of my Ford; Me walking with white pants**
**Everyone with hands in pockets, trying to act cool, Circa 1958**

Often, instead of taking our girls along with us cruisn', they would team up with some other girls and go on their own. The guys would then go together. Depending upon how many guys we had, we then decided which cars to take. It would either be Larry's '55 Buick, my '51 Ford, Bill's '40, Ford Coupe, Ron's Olds, or Ronny's '51 Merc. However, whatever car(s) we decided to take, there was always one problem that had to be ironed out: Who would sit in the coveted "shotgun," or passenger seats of the car(s) we took!

"Hey, you rode shotgun last week, Jim! It's my turn this week!" Larry exclaimed." "No, you had it last week, Larry!" Back and forth throughout the parking lot, the squabble continued between small groups of guys as they began flipping coins to see who finally nailed it down. Then off we'd go, burning rubber down the rode toward town. But there was always one major stop we had to make on the way. We needed to get gas!

Although gas was only twenty cents a gallon, we all felt obligated to pitch in for gas for the guys car we were using. Back then the places to get gas were called service stations, not gas stations. You pulled in, and a guy would come out to the driver's side and say something like, "Fill 'er up tonight, son?" "Yep, top 'er off. She's kinda low." "Check the oil too, sonny?" "Nope, oil's okay, but would you mind checking the air in the tires?" "No problem, I'll get right to it. How about the windows? Do they need cleaning?" "Yeah, you can give them a quick wash." That's why they were called service stations. Get enough gas, and they usually did all that other stuff free!

After the service station guy was all done doing his work, he'd come back to the drivers side window and say something like this, "Your gas was really low son. It took sixteen and a half gallons. That'll be three dollars and thirty cents." And we thought that was *too much!*

After filling up the car, we now headed to downtown Vallejo for a night of cruising and fun. Check out the following menu at Patches Drive-In, where the "most expensive" item on the menu back in 1958 was only sixty-five cents.

# Patches

## Drive-In
Where hungry people
Come to eat!

Located at the corner of
Tennessee and Amador Streets

## Hot Sandwiches

Bar B-Q Chicken............................................. 25c
Grilled Ham ................................................. 20c
Toasted Fried Ham........................................... 20c
Hot Dog..................................................... 20c
Grilled Cheese.............................................. 20c
Bacon & Tomato.............................................. 20c

## Cold Sandwiches

Cold Sliced Turkey.......................................... 25c
Cold Beef or Pork........................................... 20c
Cold Ham & Cheese........................................... 20c
Cold Boiled Ham............................................. 20c
Tuna ....................................................... 20c
Deviled Egg................................................. 20c

*People with*

*Hungry Appetites*

*Come to*

# Patches Drive-In

*Corner of Tennessee and Amador Streets*

## Fountain Specials

Milk Shake . . . . . . . . . . . . . . . . . . . . . . . . . . . . . . . . . . . . . . . . . 30c
    *Extra Thick* . . . . . . . . . . . . . . . . . . . . . . . . . . . . . . . . . . . . . . *40c*
Malts . . . . . . . . . . . . . . . . . . . . . . . . . . . . . . . . . . . . . . . . . . . . . 35c
All-around Shack (with Ice Cream . . . . . . . . . . . . . . . . . . . . . . . 45c
*Banana Split* a banana, 3 scoops of ice cream and toppings. . . 65c

## Refreshing Drinks

Ice Cream Sodas . . . . . . . . . . . . . . . . . . . . . . . . . . . . . . . . . . . . . . . . . . 30c
Coca-Cola . . . . . . . . . . . . . . . . . . . . . . . . . . . . . . . . . . . . . 10c and 15c
Root Beer . . . . . . . . . . . . . . . . . . . . . . . . . . . . . . . . . . . . . . 10c and 15c
Orange, Lemon or lime Ade . . . . . . . . . . . . . . . . . . . . . . . . . . . . . . 25c

Phosphate . . . . . . . . . . . . . . . . . . . . . . . . . . . . . . . . . . . . . . . . . . . . . . 25c
Cold Milk . . . . . . . . . . . . . . . . . . . . . . . . . . . . . . . . . . . . . . . . . . . . . 15c
Buttermilk . . . . . . . . . . . . . . . . . . . . . . . . . . . . . . . . . . . . . . . . . . . . . 15c
Root Beer or Coca-Cola Float . . . . . . . . . . . . . . . . . . . . . . . . . . . . . 30c
Ice Tea . . . . . . . . . . . . . . . . . . . . . . . . . . . . . . . . . . . . . . . . . . . . . . . 20c

| Freeze........35c | Pie or Cake 20c |
|---|---|
| Orange, Lime, Root Beer | A La Mode.............. 30c |

## Hot Drinks

Hot Milk . . . . . . . . . . . . . . . . . . . . . . . . . . . . . . . . . . . . . . . . . . . . . 20c
Hot Chocolate, whipped cream . . . . . . . . . . . . . . . . . . . . . . . . . . . 20c
Coffee . . . . . . . . . . . . . . . . . . . . . . . . . . . . . . . . . . . . . . . . . . . . . . 10c
Pot of Tea . . . . . . . . . . . . . . . . . . . . . . . . . . . . . . . . . . . . . . . . . . . 15c
Postum or Sanka . . . . . . . . . . . . . . . . . . . . . . . . . . . . . . . . . . . .

# From the Grill

## Hamburger...................................... 20c
With onions, lettuce, tomato, and Mayo
### With Cheese .........................................25c
## Chicken Breast on a Bun.............20c
With onions, lettuce, tomato and Mayo
### With Cheese.....................................25c

# Specials from the Grill

Hamburger Basket......................................... 50c
*Includes Hamburger, French Fries and a Coke*
Beef Burger ................................................. 50c
*Includes Chili and Beans*
Cheeseburger Basket...................................... 60c
*Includes Cheeseburger, French Fries and a Coke*
French Fries ................................................. 10c
Jumbo Fries ................................................. 15c

### Double Burger .............................30c
Includes 2 large patties
Onions, lettuce, tomato and Mayo

## We reserve the right to refuse service to anyone

## Not responsible for lost articles

If we decided to take our girls with us after leaving the Drive-In, we'd get back in our cars as they slid over next to us. No bucket seats in those days. We'd then burn rubber for downtown. The main street was Georgia Street. Up and down the street we'd go, giving a cool nod of our heads to all those we knew as we passed by. However, a few of the guys made a beeline to try to get the hottest parking spot along Georgia Street, right next to the City of Paris upscale department store. If you could get it early, you could park and watch the people walk by all night. There was only room for one car, so it came at a high premium. Everyone wanted it. Often, we'd park a car there early in the day to keep the spot. The gang who had the spot for their turn parked all evening with the radio blasting. After spending the night downtown, it was back to Eat n' Run or Patches Drive-In's for some more hang out time.

**City of Paris Department Store: Our favorite parking spot on weekend nights**

# Out of town drag strip

Racing up and down the street was another popular pass time, but the police obviously frowned upon that. Instead, we had the perfect venue just outside town. A couple miles on the outskirts of Vallejo was Columbus Parkway, a road leading to Blue Rock Springs Park, later the site of one of the infamous Zodiac murders that occurred in the Bay Area on July 4, 1969. Often, late at night some of us in the Slicks Car Club and our girlfriends would head out to the Parkway to race our cars against each other. The road was straight and exactly one-quarter of a mile, the ideal distance for a drag race. The police did patrol the area often, but if we timed it right we could get in a couple of races before they caught us.

Remember the movie Rebel Without A Cause with James Dean and Natalie Wood? In one scene, two cars lined up next to each other on a bluff getting ready to race toward a cliff overlooking the ocean. James Dean in one car, the other guy in the second. Natalie Wood stood between the two cars, then jumped high in the air giving the signal for them to race toward the cliff. The trick was to jump out of the car just before reaching the edge of the cliff. The first guy to jump would be labeled a "chicken." Those who remember the movie recall James Dean jumping out first. The other guy couldn't jump because his coat sleeve had got caught on the door handle. Over the cliff he went, the car exploding on the rocks below. We never did anything that dramatic, but in the same manner we raced down Columbus Parkway to get bragging rights.

There was this guy in town who was an automobile engineering student at a college in the Bay Area. At the time, his '55 Chevy was the hottest thing around. When he raced, he never lost. As for me and my '51 Ford? Well, it never had what it took, just a flathead V-8 that made a lot of noise. But, it was one of the coolest looking rods around, and after all, that's what counted, right?

## Ripple Wine - What a rip!...and WPLJ

None of us were old enough to drink in those days, so we couldn't go into a liquor store to buy alcohol. However, just like in the movie *American Graffiti*, we could always find a guy over twenty-one to buy us some. So we pooled what little money we had and gave it to the guy. One thing that was pretty cheap was this stuff called Ripple Wine. We heard it could really give you a *rip!* So we'd have the guy get us some Ripple, then hide behind our cars at the drive-in chugging it down. Not a bad feeling for a short time, but then the *tsunami* hit! In less than an hour, we were puking our guts out wishing we were dead!

Another thing we tried was this wine called White Port Lemon Juice. The Four Deuces, a black soul music singing group, actually did a song about the stuff called "WPLJ." It's another great song that was a part of the music we were into. Check it out on You Tube.

After drinking some of the rot gut mentioned above, somehow I'd eventually find my way home. As always, my dad would be sitting in the kitchen waiting for me. He never said a word, just the same blank stare on his face each time I came home late. I knew he was always concerned about me and my welfare. Otherwise, he wouldn't be sitting there making sure I got home safe. He just never said much. Unfortunately, we never developed a close father-son relationship. My mom once told me he had lost his parents as a very young child, and was raised by many others who didn't develop any kind of sincere relationship with him. In addition, he had actually seen his brother electrocuted and die at a construction site. He never really talked about his life as a child, but from what my mom shared, it must have been pretty tough. So I guess the whole syndrome just came along with the ride. Sadly, there wasn't much of a positive foundation in his life growing up. But he did the best he could with us, and I know he cared for me and my brother.

Anyway, off to bed I'd go, carrying my exploding head with me, looking forward to the next days adventure with no solid meaningful plans ahead for the future.

# Chapter 30

# *NEW CARS,*
# *DIFFERENT LOOKS EVERY YEAR!*

## Can't wait to see the new styles!

The Post-War era during the 50's was an exciting time for creativity and innovation. After the war ended in 1945, an industrial revolution gripped America, especially in the auto industry. Engineers and designers in Detroit were encouraged to allow their creative juices to flow, and man, did they flow!

Today, most automobiles represent nothing more than miniature cookie-cutter-dough, stamped out of the same mold. Look at the cars on the road today and you'll see basically the same body styles with different names on the side, all overpriced. If it wasn't for the name on the car, it would be hard to decipher one from another. Poor manufacturing, constant recalls, very little chrome or pizzaz, midget sizes, and computerized systems that cost a fortune to replace if they fail. Not much creativity, but plenty of hype to buy these shiny pieces of dough made of cheap material so thin one need only lean on them to inflict a dent. I get a kick out of watching some of the TV auto commercials. Here's one you'll recognize: First, a group of young people are sitting at an outdoor restaurant fooling with their smart phones (not personally interacting with each other, of course). Next, a bright red auto just off the assembly line drives by slowly, silhouetted against a grey background to make it stand out. All of a sudden, the participants in the commercial become "mind struck" and speechless by the utter vivid beauty of this red jelly bean driving by. Then comes the sales pitch.

Now switch to a different channel and see a similar commercial with another jelly bean that looks almost the same as the one in the first commercial. But it's not. It's a different brand altogether with more people gawking at it. How do we know the car is different? Well, it actually has a different name on the side. But there's another more important piece of information we're given. We're actually *told* what it is. Wouldn't want to keep us "dumb Americans" in the dark about the name of the car now, would they?! But some of us are still pretty dumb, right? So to make sure we don't mistake the second car for the ten others out there that may look like it, a few "mind-blowing" major changes have been made. How about that brand new tail light cover. Now there's something we've been hearing about coming for a year. Or what about that brand new genuine leather steering wheel cover, or maybe even an extra hidden button you can now engage from three hundred yards away to open your trunk before you reach your vehicle. All to make certain that fabulous stamped out gem can now be advertised as a real "authentic" original with all "new" creative innovative features. Don't want to get confused about what we're buying, right? But many are still "stamped" out of the same plastic mold with just a few minor changes.

Most applaud the creativity in the auto industry today and say it has evolved into a continuous emerging marvel. That may be true if you've got the big bucks to buy those expensive marvels. But what about the normal American buyer with monthly payments for something his family needs and can only afford? True, things have evolved, but with one distinct caveat: Backwards and More Expensive!

# Well built classics

The 50's and early 60's ushered in a period of creative well-built classic cars that have stood the test of time. Most were made of metal, had plenty of chrome and style, and were strong! They're just as beautiful today as they were when they rolled off the assembly line. Detroit released new and exciting models each year. Whether it was Chevy, Ford, Olds, Pontiac, Buick, Mercury, Plymouth, Dodge, or Chrysler, we could always expect exciting innovative changes to occur in the industry. It may sound crazy, but we couldn't wait to see what new looks were about to be released each year. Detroit never disappointed. Today, the results can be seen at any classic car show across America, a true example of *American Graffiti*. Some of us were lucky enough to be there during those times and experience that "classic car" revolution.

# Chapter 31

# *THE ACCIDENT : PHIL, ERNIE, JOJO*

**Early photo of one of our junior high basketball teams. My best friend Phil is No. 20. I'm No. 24. This photo was taken a few years before the terrible automobile accident described below.**

## High School class reunion photo: The "Black Line"

Our class graduated in 1958. Each time I've attended our class reunion, there's a picture of our class on the wall. All classmates who've died have their photo's highlighted with a "black line" around them. I'm always drawn to two photos. Phil Draper was my best friend in school. Ernie Sickler was another friend. Both are outlined in black.


## Planning for the big dance party

Phil was a great athlete in both basketball and baseball. We did everything together. His folks and mine were also very close. Ernie was another friend I hung around with. JoJo was a younger friend of ours.

Ernie and I had spent Friday, March 21, 1958, cruising around, talking about a dance party the four of us were going to Saturday night, March 22, 1958, up in Fairfield, about twenty miles away. Phil's dad was going to let him use his car, so we were all jacked up about going. I would be the last to be picked up before we took off. Phil called me about six o'clock in the evening that Saturday. "Hey, Orr, we'll be over to pick you up in about a half hour."


## Ever pray when you were a kid?

I prayed a lot when I was a kid, the type of prayers most of us probably prayed. "Help me not to die, God. Help my mom and dad. Help my little brother or sister. Now I lay me down to sleep, I pray the Lord my soul to keep. Our Father, who art in Heaven . . . God, please don't let the atomic bomb go off over my head!" You know, things like that.

Although I was raised a Catholic, I didn't know much about God. I hated going to church, listening to all that Latin stuff. All those rituals made no sense to me at all, but my brother and I were forced to go. I even made up sins to confess to the priest in the confessional just to get in and out quickly. However, I believed God existed and prayed to him a lot. I just didn't know if he was listening. Looking back, I know he was that fateful night in 1958.

## Now I know what hot means, mommy!

When we were all very young, most of us probably hung around the kitchen while our moms were cooking. My mom would always say something like, "Don't touch that stove, Jimmy. It's hot!" But in spite of her warnings, I didn't know what "hot" meant. When I got near the stove, I maybe sensed some type of warm feeling, but "hot," what the hell did that mean? I'm sure most of us trusted and believed what our moms told us was true, but some of us just couldn't resist touching that stove to see what she meant. Once we touched it and got our little pinkies seared, we were instantly converted from believers to *knowers!* We then *knew* what "hot" meant! On that eventful Saturday night in 1958, I went from believing God existed to *knowing* he was real!

**Phil and I hang'n out at Conn Dam, five months before his horrific accident**

## Sorry Phil, think I'll pass on the party tonight

When Phil called that Saturday night, at the last moment I decided not to go. "Phil, I think I'll pass tonight, buddy." Phil couldn't understand why I changed my mind. The four of us had planned it for some time, and were looking forward to going. He kept trying to persuade me to change my mind. "Sorry, Phil, I just feel like staying home." "Okay, Jim, I'll call you tomorrow and let you know how it went, but you'll be sorry you didn't make it."

Can't remember how I first found out about the accident Sunday morning. We did get the Sunday paper delivered to our doorstep early in the morning, so possibly my mom saw the article, then let us all know as we woke up. The lead story on the front page of the *Vallejo Times Herald* was dramatic, painting a vivid picture of the horrible accident that took place as Phil, Ernie, and JoJo were driving back from the party. Phil was driving, Ernie was in the front passenger seat. We later found out JoJo was asleep in the back seat.

The article in Sunday mornings paper read as follows :

*The Vallejo Times-Herald*
SOLANO COUNTY'S MORNING NEWSPAPER
HOME OF MARE ISLAND NAVAL SHIPYARD
SUNDAY, MARCH 23, 1958
YOUTH 17, INFANT KILLED IN U.S. 40 CRASH

# Vallejo Boy, Infant Dead In Crash Here

## Six Others Are Injured In Rindler Hill Pileup

A 17 year old Vallejo youth and a 15 day old baby were killed and six others injured at 11:00 PM last night on rain swept Highway 40 near Rindler Hill in a violent three car collision. Dead on arrival at Kaiser Hospital were ERNEST SICKLER, 17 of 117 Hollywood Street, Vallejo, and Kevin Ray Pistourius, the 15 day old son of Mr. and Mrs. Raymond Pistourius, of Woodland. The baby's parents were critically injured and were taken to Travis Air Force Base hospital.

OTHERS INJURED were the baby's grandfather, William Finney, 53 of Woodland, PHIL DRAPER, 16, of 117 El Monte Street, Vallejo, Dan Karabedian, 16, of 824 Florida Street, Vallejo, and Ben Deandra of Dixon.

Deandra and Karabedian were not seriously injured.

The accident took place at eleven o'clock on Saturday night, March 22, 1958. Phil, Ernie, and JoJo were returning from the party. It was raining when Phil's car swerved across the double line, striking the other vehicle head on as it was traveling north. The collision was so violent it tore the engine out of Phil's dad's '53 Chevy and flung it across the road. Ernie was riding in the passenger seat up front - *the seat I would have been in if I had gone with them.* He was killed instantly. JoJo was asleep in the back seat and woke up in a field with minimal injuries. A young infant in the other vehicle was also killed, its parents critically injured. As for Phil, he was paralyzed from the neck down, a quadriplegic for life. On the positive side, Phil eventually became president of the National Quadriplegic Association. On the negative side, Phil's parents never got over the ordeal. With all the pain, despair, and law suits, they eventually divorced. Phil died at an early age.

Phil and Ernie's high school graduation photos were taken in early March of 1958 for our high school yearbook. The horrific accident took place shortly after on March 22, 1958.

# Chapter 32

# *THE "SLICKS" DANCE :*
# *CASA DE VALLEJO HOTEL*

**Casa de Vallejo Hotel ~ Venue for the "Slicks" dance party**

## The Big Dance

Sometime back in '59 or '60, our "Slicks" car club decided to put on a big dance party with a rock and roll band. All the members met to decide how to pull it off. Because our club was so popular around town, we figured a dance might be a big success. Besides using some of the club dues money, we decided to sell tickets. We also found a great band in the area to play for us. In addition, we needed a place to have the dance. After checking things out, we made a deal with the Casa de Vallejo Hotel in Vallejo. It was the best hotel in town and would be the perfect venue. However, we needed to sell a lot of tickets to cover the hotel, band, and all the expenses. Each of us canvassed the town and surrounding areas selling all the tickets we could. Didn't know how the idea was going to come off, but the guys and girls around town thought it had a great chance of succeeding. As we anticipated, the tickets sold out quickly and we started planning for the big event.

## "Out of Town" Judy shows up: "Jim, will you take me?"

My girlfriend Ruth and I had recently broken off our relationship, so I decided to go stag. Just a quick story about that before I continue. I was working nights at the *Vallejo Times Herald* newspaper at the time. Unaware of it, I would go to work, then Ruth began hooking up with this other guy in town behind my back. One day I dropped by her house to say hi to her mom. "How's Ruth doing these days?" I asked. Her mom replied, "Oh, we just found out she and her boyfriend went off and got married." "Married! are you kidding me?" "Yep, we haven't heard from them in a while." I never heard anything about her after that. But back to the dance at the Casa de Vallejo.

About a week before the dance, this cool-looking girl came up to me one day and said, "Hey, Jim, are you taking anyone to the dance next Saturday night?" I responded, "No, I'm not taking anyone." She then said, "Would you like to take me?" Caught off guard, I paused a bit, then said, "Well, yeah, I guess so." Her name was Judy. She told me she was new in town, had heard about the dance, and was hoping someone would invite her. "I'll give you my phone number, Jim. Give me a call, and we'll get together before the dance." "Okay, Judy, I'll get back to you."

## Something odd about this girl?

Judy and I got together a couple times before the dance, but I noticed something different about her. Couldn't put my finger on it, but I felt like I was being used for something other than just simply striking up a new friendship. In spite of my misgivings, I went along for the ride as we made plans for Saturday night. The night of the dance finally arrived, and after helping set up things at the hotel, I picked her up, and we headed back. We were both excited about what was going be a night of fun and dancing. Man, was I in for a big surprise!

## Judy doesn't come back

After arriving at the hotel, I introduced Judy to some friends just as the band began playing. The place started rockin' and everyone was in a groove having a great time. After our first dance, Judy excused herself to go to the bathroom. "Wait here, Jim. I'll be right back." So I waited a long time for her to return, but she never came back. With the place packed and everyone dancing, I began looking for her. Next thing I know, I looked across the dance floor, and this "new girl in town" was dancing with another guy, who was also a member of the Slicks. After the band stopped playing, I went over to both of them and asked, "Hey, what's up with this?" After attempting to get an explanation and being completely ignored, I finally got the picture. "Out-of-Town Judy" simply used me to get her butt into the dance! She obviously had other plans, having no intention of spending the evening with me, but rather looking to get hooked up with this other guy. No wonder she seemed so aloof and distant the few hours we spent together days before the dance. After a few lighthearted words back and forth between the three of us, I almost come to blows with my fellow club member. But discretion prevailed as I kept my cool, accepting the unfortunate occurrence.

No big deal. The band was still rockin', the night was young, and there were plenty of other loose chicks around. What else could possibly go wrong?.... *Plenty!*

## "The Cyclists' Raid"

"The Cyclists' Raid," published in the January 1951 Harpers Magazine, is a story about an American Motorcycle Association rally that got out of hand in Hollister, California, on the weekend of July 4, 1947. *The Wild One*, starring Marlon Brando, is a 1953 film considered the original outlaw biker film examining motorcycle gang violence, based upon the legend of the Hollister Riot.

## The Hell's Angels - Unwanted guests arrive!

The well-known Hell's Angels is a motorcycle club that began in Fontana, California, around 1948. They had affiliate clubs all over the state. Back in the 50's, one of those clubs just happened to be in Vallejo. Its members were known for their bizarre and violent behavior. We were about to experience a piece of that behavior at our Slicks dance party.

Even though Out-of-Town Judy ditched me early, I managed to hook up with another girl, and we were having a blast. While we were dancing and in a solid groove, all hell broke loose near the hotel front door. Like I said, what else could possibly go wrong? We were about to find out what that *what else* was!

## Ride Hard, Die Fast!

Suddenly, in burst a large group of tough-looking guys dressed in black jackets and Nazi helmets. "Hells Angels: Vallejo Chapter - Ride Hard, Die Fast" embroidered on the back of their jackets. The band stopped playing as these apes began pushing themselves through the crowd. No way we were going to put up with this. A confrontation took place, and the fight began! I managed to lay a good one on the chin of one of these boneheads, when suddenly a loud *bang* blasted out from the center of the room. White dust and pieces of the ceiling began falling. We then realized one of these retards shot his gun into the ceiling!

The girls began screaming and people started running for the exits. The Vallejo Police finally arrived and broke up what was left of our unwanted guests, sending them on their way, but not before arresting the drunken Hell's Angel idiot who shot the gun. The crowd then returned to the dance floor. The band cranked it up again, and it was on with the dance after the slight interruption.

# Chapter 33

## *THE PARTY,*
## *THE SHOTGUN BLAST, THE STOCKADE!*

### Hey, Jim, wanna go to a party?

It was a hot Friday night that summer in 1959 as a bunch of us guys met up at Patches Drive-In to hang out. After a while, my friend Ron and another guy drove up in Ron's cool '51 Mercury.

"Hey, Jim, I hear there's a party someplace up on Tuolumne Street. Want to check it out with us?" "Sure," I responded. So I jumped in the back seat as Ron introduced me to his older cousin Arnie, who had just moved into town. We then burned rubber down the road, first gear, second gear, third gear, the mufflers blowing out a cool rumbling sound that echoed off the sides of the buildings we passed. As we drove along,

I noticed something weird about Ron's cousin Arnie. He never spoke a word, having this glassy-eyed, tough-guy angry look painted on his face as we motored along. He continued to remain cold and aloof as Ron and I jawed back and forth with each other.

## Sorry guys, you need an invitation!

Ron didn't know for sure where the party was, but after driving around a while, we finally recognized some cars parked outside a house. "Hey, that's Lawrences' house." "Yeah, I know Lawrence. The party must be at his place."

We then parked, got out, and walked up to the front door. After ringing the door bell, a girl greeted us. "Hey guys, got your invitations?" "No, but we know Lawrence from school. Any chance of coming in?" "Sorry, it's a private party. You need an invitation!" She then abruptly slammed the door in our faces. At that, Arnie became extremely angry, and bolted off. We all three then jumped back into Ron's Merc, and left. In an angry rage, Arnie exclaimed, "Take me back to my house....now!"

## What's that thing under Arnie's arm?

Upon arriving at Arnie's house, he vaulted out of the car. "Wait here, I need to get something." Five minutes later, he came running back. Ron and I then suddenly noticed something that looked like a rifle tucked under his right arm. "Its a sawed-off shotgun, Ron!" "What the hell?!" Arnie then quickly yanked the door open and jumped in. Frozen in disbelief, Ron finally said, "Arnie, what are you going to do?" "I'm going to get us into that party. Get going!" I then asked him, "What do you mean, Arnie?" Arnie responded, "Like I said, we're getting into that party. Get moving!" Scared he was maybe going shoot us, we complied, and headed back to the party.

Why we didn't try to stop him, I'll never know. We were both scared to death, for sure! Or maybe we thought he was just joking. Call it fate or whatever, but the frightful event that was about to occur that night would actually affect my life in an extremely positive and unique manner. As Ron and I continued looking at each other in shock, Arnie continued to bark orders at us. "Come on, get going....burn rubber!"

After what seemed like an eternity, we arrived back at the party. All along I was thinking, *Is this really happening? Is this psycho going to do something weird? Is he only kidding, just trying to act like a tough guy? What should we do?"*

Once at the party, Arnie leaped out, then ran toward the front door with shotgun in hand. Ron then said, "Hey, Jim, I think he's going to do something stupid." With that, I immediately ran to a window and looked in. I saw Bill, one of my high school friends, dancing with his girlfriend Bev. You couldn't miss him; he was a big guy, and one of Vallejo High's star football players. I then began pounding on the window, trying to get his attention. He finally saw me and came to the window. "Hey, Jim, what's up?" "Bill, there's this crazy guy outside who has a shotgun, and says he's going to...." Suddenly, *BANG!* A loud blast echoed through the air from near the front of the house. Still scared, I ran back to Ron's Merc and jumped in. Ron and Arnie were already in the car. None of us spoke a word as we barreled down the road, dropping off "Shotgun Arnie" at his place.

## Gotta get a fool-proof alibi!

As we continued driving around, I asked Ron,"What should we do?" Ron then said, "Hey, we don't want to be hooked up with this thing. What we need is a fool-proof alibi, one that places us someplace else." I then responded, "Why do we need an alibi, all Arnie did was shoot the gun into the air?" "Air, my ass!" Ron exclaimed. "I saw him shoot the gun through the front door!" "Are you kidding?" With that, I made a very astute and highly intelligent decision: "Okay, let's start working on that fool-proof alibi right now!"

## The "Alibi Girls" up in Napa

We then drove out to Blue Rock Springs Park in Vallejo and parked, planning our next brilliant move. After talking about our options, Ron said, "Hey, I've got a great idea, let's drive up to Napa. I know some girls up there. They could say we spent the whole evening with them." "Okay, sounds good. Let's go!" In our haste to come up with our fool-proof alibi, we had forgotten one minor point. There were at least ten people who saw us at the party! Talk about dumb! Nonetheless, that was the plan as we raced toward Napa.

During the thirteen-mile ride, we talked about what had occurred, including all the clever points that would anchor our fool-proof alibi. Ron figured some of the girls he knew might be hanging out at A&W Root Beer Drive-In. He was right. Just as we drove in, there were some girls he knew sitting in a car. We went over and Ron began talking to one of them.

"Hey, Jackie, we've been in a little trouble down in Vallejo. No big deal, but if anything ever came of it, would you girls mind saying we were up here with all of you?" Without hesitating, Jackie responded, "Sure, Ronny, no sweat." With our fool-proof alibi now firmly established, we drove back to Vallejo and cruised around a bit, ending up back at Patches Drive-In Restaurant.

## Whadda ya mean, "The police are looking for us?"

While driving into Patches, Johnnie, one of the guys in the Slicks, saw us, then came over and said, "Hey, where have you guys been all night? Did you know the cops were looking for you?" "Why? We didn't do anything." "Didn't you hear what happened?" "No," we replied. Johnnie then uttered the words that sent chills up and down our spines: "The guy who had the party, was shot!" Reality suddenly sank in! What we didn't know was that when Psycho Arnie unloaded the shotgun pellets through the door, Lawrence was just about to open it. Fortunately, he was reaching across the door as the gun went off, causing only splinters from the door to injure his arm. Thank God he wasn't standing in front of the door when the pellets barreled through!

After hearing what actually occurred, Ron and I decided it was best to drive directly to the Vallejo Police Department on Marin Street, the first rational decision we'd made all night! As we drove there, we had no idea what was about to happen. Neither of us had ever been in any serious trouble before. Nothing to worry about right?....*Wrong!*

During the drive to the Police Department, Ron and I discussed what we would tell them. We had nothing to do with it, tried to persuade Arnie not to do anything stupid, and thought he might shoot us. I also tried to warn people in the house what might happen. So we were turning ourselves in, and not trying to evade the issue, plus a number of other things that were clearly in our favor. Nothing to worry about, right? They were bound to let us go. Wrong *again*! In our irrational exuberance, we had forgotten one thing: *We had left the scene of a serious crime!*

We drove up to the Police Department, parked in front, got out, and walked up the cold marble steps through the front door. Above the door etched in marble read an old axiom theorized by the ancient Greek historian Herodotus, 485 BC - c. 425 BC.

"THOUGH FREE, THEY ARE NOT ABSOLUTELY FREE,
FOR THEY HAVE A MASTER OVER THEM, THE LAW"

As we entered the Police Department, were we about to find out just how true that ancient axiom was! We walked in and told the officer on duty who we were. Immediately, two other officers came in and slapped handcuffs on us. I then said, "We didn't do anything, officer. What's the problem?" "Oh, no problem at all, son. You're both just going to be charged as accomplices to an assault with a deadly weapon, with intent to cause great bodily harm, that's all!"...."I want my Mommy!"

The officer also told us they had arrested Arnie as well. We were then read our rights: "You have the right to remain silent. If you give up that right, anything you say may be used against you in a court of law. You also have the right to an attorney. You two punks want to talk about this now or not?" "Uh, yes, sir, I think we'd like to talk about it now!"

## The Stockade!

After all the finger printing and processing, Ron and I were placed in separate jail cells. I was put in a cell with an old drunk who was in real bad shape and smelled like the bottom of a bird cage. The sound of the bars slamming behind me was sudden and final. I had never been in this kind of trouble before, but was obviously now in a serious fix. After a while, my folks came to see me. Mom was really upset, but dad kinda accepted the matter without saying much. The next mornings headline in the *Vallejo Times Herald* newspaper read "Three Punks Shoot Young Man at Local Party!"

Didn't sleep much that first night in jail. Next morning, the jailer brought in breakfast, a few Rice Krispies floating around in a bowl of skim milk. Shortly after, the old man in the cell with me was taken out. I never saw him again. Then a really bizarre thing happened.

I was sitting on the edge of the bed when a loud noise happened. All of a sudden, the door to my cell opened all the way. I walked out, and looked up and down the hallway, but there was no one around. "Have I been miraculously delivered from this place?" The door at the end of the hallway then opened, and out stepped this officer. "What the hell are you doing out here?" he exclaimed. "Don't know, officer. The door just opened on its own." "Get your ass back in there!" He then left, and the cell door slammed shut. Must have been some kind of malfunction - kinda like our original plan to drive up to Napa for that solid fool-proof alibi, the one we had obviously already trashed and forgot about. However, those cute little alibi girls up in Napa hadn't forgotten. That segment about this story was about to soon backfire on us!

# The Arraignment

The arraignment was set for the next morning. My folks retained a well-respected attorney in town to help me out. That morning Ron and I were led into the courtroom, then seated in a box overlooking the gallery. Ron's cousin Arnie wasn't anywhere to be seen. In fact, we never saw him again. He apparently had some kind of criminal record, and was prosecuted under a different set of guidelines. It was now time to hear the charges levied against us, but that wasn't all that was about to happen. Waiting just around corner was the big surprise coming Ron and I had forgotten about. Remember those notorious *Alibi Girls* up in Napa? They were about to arrive on the scene!

As we sat waiting for the judge to appear, suddenly the Napa *Alibi Girls* all walked into court! If you recall, these were the sweet young things that promised to perjure themselves on our behalf! They were about to tell the judge we were up in Napa the whole evening with them when the incident occurred. After entering the courtroom, they sashayed straight up the aisle and sat down right in the front row, winking at us as if to say, "Don't worry, boys, we've got your butts covered." Ron and I looked at each other and thought, *Great, this is all we need - especially since we've already confessed, not withstanding the fact that we were seen by others at the party.*

At that point, we subtly tried to get the girls attention, motioning with our heads and hands in an effort to tell them, "Shut up! Don't say anything!" But they continued sitting there with these sly Cheshire cat smiles on their faces, ready to lie for these nice innocent Vallejo boys displayed on stage in front of them. Finally, the smile on one of their faces disappeared. She then turned to the girl next to her and mumbled something. The other girl's smile also disappeared. They both then looked back at Ron and I, and nodded their heads as if to say, "Okay, we've got it. We'll shut up." Ron and I finally breathed sighs of relief, then sat back to wait for the judge to appear.

The judge then walked into the courtroom. "Please stand, the honorable Judge Thomas, in and for the County of Solano, State of California, now presiding. Please be seated." Because Ron and I were nineteen, we were both about to be arraigned as adults for a very serious felony crime.

I'm sure I must have prayed somewhere along the way during the ordeal, like "God, help me!" Well, in his miraculous way, God was working in the courtroom that day in a way I could never truly comprehend. As strange as it may seem, the perfect judge had been assigned to preside over our case. Ironically, years later, that same judge and I would cross paths again under much more positive and very unique circumstances.

## Saved by the bell!

Because I had no criminal record, my attorney petitioned the court to process my case in juvenile court. In those days, there was a California statute that allowed this, but it was up to the judge to grant the petition or not. Judge Tom decided to do so. I was then remanded to juvenile court and released to my parents custody. My case was then referred to the Solano County Probation Department for a pre-sentence report. It was assigned to a young Juvenile Probation Officer named Ken, who had just graduated from college and began working for the department. It was his responsibility to submit a report to the court with a recommendation regarding what my sentence should be. After all the background checks, interviews with me, my parents, character witnesses, etc., he recommended I be placed on one-year juvenile probation. Judge Tom accepted his recommendation. But this unique story in my life doesn't end here.

As I mentioned above, my path would again miraculously cross with Judge Tom as well as the young Probation Officer Ken years later.

One of the real ironic and bizarre things about the incident is that I was actually employed by the *Vallejo Times Herald* newspaper at the time. When I was released to my parents custody, the paper allowed me to keep my night job during the court proceedings, but I was treated and ridiculed badly by most of the older adults on the night shift who actually knew very little about what happened during the incident. But, there was one guy I remember who was always coming to my rescue and supporting me. Obviously, he must have been in a little trouble at one time in his life, and had some empathy for what I might be going through. I really appreciated his help during those long nights cleaning the presses.

## Record Expunged - Yippee!

In those days, there was a specific California statute that allowed adults to "expunge," or completely eliminate any record of criminal activity that occurred as a juvenile. In order to do so, you had to be twenty-one, and have no criminal convictions since originally being placed on probation. Since that was my case, once I turned twenty-one, I petitioned the Solano County Superior Court to expunge my record, and it was granted. This option would be extremely important in my future in that it allowed me to eventually become employed in the criminal justice system as guess what...a Deputy Probation Officer!

However, not only that, but also with the same Solano County Probation Department, and working for the same judge who presided over my case as a juvenile....and for the same Probation Officer Ken who processed my case in juvenile court years earlier!

# THE LATER YEARS

## Chapter 34

### NOTE TO THE READER

Chapters 34 - 36 and the following Post Script stories were added because this is an "Autobiography" of my life to the present. Please consider reading on. I believe you'll find some of the information interesting and possibly relative in some ways to your own life experiences. Either way, I sincerely hope you've enjoyed the book up to this point.

## *HANG'N OUT, NO DIRECTION, NO PLANS*

### Be an Engineer, son

I served the year on probation, but had no concrete plans. My dad always said, "Be an engineer, son, they make lots of money." I thought he meant be one of those guys who drives a train! He never provided any information about what an engineer did. He just saw them where he worked at Mare Island Shipyard. They wore white shirts, ties, made lots of money, drove nice cars, and didn't get their hands dirty. So, that was obviously the job for his son. Only one problem: He knew nothing about how to become one nor did he bother to look into it. Just "become one" was his fruitless advice. He never realized it took at least four years of college or more, plus a solid foundation in math before even pursuing such a career, not withstanding the cost of such an education. So, without any plans, I hung around with my Slicks buddies, worked odd jobs, partied on the weekends, and generally led a rudderless life.

## Junior College

Eventually, I decided to do something to improve myself, so I began attending junior college. I had no idea what classes to take. I always liked to draw and paint, so thought I might enjoy something oriented to a profession requiring such skills, like maybe becoming an architect. So one day I met with a college counselor to find out the courses required for such a profession. Unfortunately, he was no help, telling me my lack of serious application in high school would hinder me from pursuing such a field, and that I should forget it altogether. Really helpful! I always felt I was smart enough to do better, but never received any meaningful encouragement or direction from my parents. But there was one teacher in high school who suggested I pursue studies in English. She thought I'd do well at it. Not for me at the time, though. I didn't enjoy school that much, except for sports. The rest of the time it was girls, fast cars, and hanging out with my buddies in the Slicks Car Club. So, I continued wandering aimlessly, taking classes just to pass the time.

# Opportunity knocks: Take it or not?

Then one day in 1960 I ran into this guy Bill I knew in high school. We started yakking and he told me he was going up to the Napa State Hospital Mental Institution the following week to take a written test to become a Psychiatric Technician. "What's that?" I asked. "They work with the mentally ill in a hospital setting. Why not come up with me and take the test?" "No thanks, Bill, I wouldn't dig working at that nut house!" "Okay, but why not just come along with me for the ride if you're not doing anything next Tuesday?" I figured, what the heck, I wasn't doing anything that day, so I decided to go along. "Sure, Bill, I'll go up with you." "Great, Jim, I'll call you, and we'll plan it."

# Okay, I'll give it a shot

The following Tuesday Bill and I made the trip to Napa State Hospital. Once there, we went into a room with others filling out applications. "Come on, Jim, just sign up and take the damn thing. Even if you passed, you wouldn't need to go any farther." "Okay, what the heck, I'll take it."

We filled out our applications and gave them to the lady in charge. "Wait here, boys, while I process these." After a while, she came back and told us our applications had been accepted. "Have a seat over there. We'll call you in about fifteen minutes." She then came back and began calling out names. Bill, me, and several others were then led into a second room to be oriented about the job and take the written test. After hearing the details, I thought, *Man, I don't want any part of this!* But since I was there, why not take the test just to see what happens? Although I wasn't excited about working in such a place, if by some chance I passed and got the job, maybe I could handle it. Besides, I was living at home, not working at anything steady, and could use the money to fix up the old '51 Ford.

So Bill and I took the test, then drove back to Vallejo to await the results.


## Dear Mr. Orr, you passed!

Two weeks later, a letter came from the California Department of Mental Hygiene. "Dear Mr. Orr, you passed the written test for the position of Psychiatric Technician. Call Napa State Hospital to confirm your interview." "What!" I couldn't believe it. I then called Bill. "Hey, buddy, I guess we're going to become Psychiatric Technicians, huh?" Bill responded, "Not me, Jim, I *failed* the damn thing!" So by coincidence I got invited to take a test for a job I wanted no part of, yet passed, whereas Bill, who had done all the research and wanted the job badly, ended up failing. Go figure.


## Now I'm a Psychiatric Technician

I'll never forget my first day on the job at the Mental Institution at Napa State Hospital. I dropped by the administrative office and picked up my "ward keys," and was assigned to this hospital ward way in back of the hospital grounds, T-16. I drove there, parked, walked up to the door, then slipped the heavy metal key into the slot. The door creaked open, and I locked it behind me. I then turned around and looked down the hallway. "What the hell have I gotten myself into?!"

Anybody remember the movie One Flew Over the Cuckoo's Nest? Look it up. I was right smack in the middle of it! These were locked wards with a variety of patients suffering from a myriad of mental illnesses I still hadn't learned much about: schizophrenia, dementia, dissociative disorders, anxiety attacks, obsessive-compulsive disorders, manic depressive disorders, hebephrenia, catatonic disorders, hallucinations, delusions, including many dangerous patients, most spaced out on drugs and often receiving electric shock therapy once a week. A real *Snake Pit* in those early days.

As I was being examined by all the patients while walking down the hall to the nursing station, I tried to project a kind and caring attitude toward each of them I passed. But at the same time I was still thinking, *What am I doing here? Time to make a decision. Turn around and leave? Or stay?* I had just bought a cool '57 Chevy. Needed money for payments, plus I wanted to customize it. *So....think I'll stay!*

After some time, I finally got accustomed to the routine of the job and what was expected. In addition, I was physically strong and in pretty good shape. As a result, I was recruited to work on one of the two maximum security wards in the hospital where the most dangerous patients were located. Only qualified and fit personnel were selected for the assignment. It was actually looked upon as a coveted position, desired by many, with very few being chosen for the assignment. However, it was not as dangerous as it seemed, as long you knew the hazards, kept your antennas up, worked closely with your other physically fit coworkers, and never let your guard down. Rarely any of our staff got hurt. However, there was one incident during my assignment on the maximum security ward that occurred in the Fall of 1962....one I'll never forget!

Eddie Machin, one of the most well-known heavy weight boxers in the world, was arrested in the Fall of 1962 one night in Vallejo, California, while clinically depressed and wandering on a bridge threatening to commit suicide. He was taken directly to the maximum security ward where I worked. I just happened to be off that night. As he was admitted, he became violent and began using my co workers as punching bags, injuring several of them. The next evening when I arrived at work, I became aware of what had occurred. At that time, Eddie was in full restraint on a bed in a side room. I went into the room to talk with him and see how he was doing. Kindly, I said, "Hello, Eddie, my name is Jim. I'm very sorry all this happened to you. We're going to do all we can to help you get through this ordeal." He then looked straight up at me with this angry look on his face and said one thing: "I'm going to kill you!"

I believe it may have been at that moment I decided to become a full-time college student, pursue some form of degree, and consider another profession. With that, while working nights at the hospital, I attended college at San Francisco State College during the days.

Eddie Machin was found dead in San Francisco on August 8, 1972, apparently the result of a fall from a second-story apartment window. He was forty years old. It was not known if the cause of his death was suicide, an accident, or murder.

## Suddenly more "studious," - Then Nursing School

After a couple years at the hospital, I was offered a scholarship to attend nursing school. I hadn't ever thought about becoming a Registered Nurse, but the opportunity came along, so I took advantage of it. After graduating from the Santa Rosa Junior College School of Nursing in 1963, I stayed at the hospital for a few years, continuing my education at San Francisco State College, graduating in 1966 with a degree in Health Science. At that point, I began making plans to leave Nursing for another career.

**CITY LEAGUE BASKETBALL TEAM AT NAPA STATE HOSPITAL**
**Author Jim Orr, front row center.**

Napa sponsored a City Basketball League. Evening games, electronic scoreboards, referees, big crowds, and plenty of coverage in the local newspaper sports news section. I contacted the coaches of the hospital team and asked if I could try out. I made the team, and played the entire City League season. We had a great team, and competed a couple evenings a week. Although we were eliminated in the first playoffs, we had a strong team, and competed in the City League for several seasons thereafter. In addition, the hospital sponsored a City League "fast pitch" softball baseball team. I played on that team as well.

However, our softball team didn't enjoy as much success as our basketball team did.

# Natives Down Kaiser, YC's Beat Squires

Native Sons downed Kaiser Steel 66-53, Imola defeated Wards 45-41, and Yates beat Squires 84-47 in City League Basketball play last night in the Redwood and Ridgeview gyms.

Imola led Wards 21-14 at the half. Jim Orr had 18 for Imola, Terry Henley 11, Jim Dillard 6, Jack Wavery 4, Jim Coleman 3, George Cabot 2, Ed Nivens 1.

**Napa Register - City League - Oct. 18, 1961**

# Imola Downs YC's In CBL Game, 65-52

Imola beat Yates-Cochrane 65-52, Norwalk defeated DeMolay 58-28, Squires beat Has Beens 45-28, and Ivy's won over Arden's on forfeit in City League games last night.

Imola led the YC's 42-26 at the half. Terry Henley led Imola with 24 points, followed by Jim Orr with 15, Jim Dillard with 10, George Cabot with 9, Dick Woodworth with 3, and W. Donlin and B. Thomas with 2 each.

**Napa Register - City League - Oct. 25, 1961**

**Jim Orr, left, of Imola, is out at first as Joe Harris of Napa Grocery Center takes throw during City Softball League game last night at fairgrounds won by NGC 16-2. League opened play last night with Sports beating Gordon 2-0 in the other game of the doubleheader. ( Register Photo )**

**Hang'n with two friends at Napa State Hospital**
**Tommy and my 57' Chevy**

## Time for something else: Pharmaceutical Rep?

As stated earlier, I stayed at Napa State Hospital for a few years, graduating from college in 1966. However, I desired something else. Because I had experience as a Registered Nurse, plus a degree in Health Science, I felt I might do well as a pharmaceutical representative for a major drug company. I started checking out this option. Interestingly, the regional manger for Sandoz Pharmaceuticals lived just across town from me in Napa. I contacted him and told him about my qualifications. We set up a meeting, and he took me with him on sales calls to various physicians' offices and clinics on "Pill Hill" in Oakland, California. I was eventually offered a position with the company, which included a good salary, company car, good benefits, expense account, and more. I made plans to resign from the hospital, but then one day I heard a loud knock on my front door.

## Hi Jim, my name is Uncle Sam. Got a minute?

I went to the door and answered it. Standing there was this old man with a white beard dressed in red, white, and blue. I asked him what he wanted. "Jim, my name is Uncle Sam. Can I have a minute of your time? I'd like to discuss somethimg very important with you."

WHAT?

**You're mine, Jim!**

# Chapter 35

# *VIETNAM: "YOU'RE MINE, JIM!"*

## Police action? Are you kidding?

During 1966, American military casualties were mounting up fast in this "skirmish" originally referred to as a "police action" way off in a place called Vietnam. The conflict was initiated to stem the tide of North Vietnamese Communist rule into South Vietnam.

Medical personnel were needed badly. Shortly after Uncle Sam talked to me on my door step, I received this letter. "Dear Mr. Orr, please report to the local Army Induction Center in San Francisco. You've been drafted into the Army Nurse Corps for the next two years!"

## THE GOOD, THE BAD, THE UGLY

Remember the spaghetti Western movie with actor Clint Eastwood, *The Good, The Bad, and The Ugly*? It was released in 1966. Ironically, I was drafted into the army that same year! For me, Vietnam represented all three aspects of that movie - *The Good, The Bad, and The Ugly!*

## *THE GOOD:* Warrant Officer - The ideal rank

Because I had a college degree, I was given the option of entering one of two branches of the service, either the Army Nurse Corp for two years, designated as a Warrant Officer, or the Medical Service Corp for three years, eventually attaining the rank of Captain. I didn't want either, so I took the shorter term, and was processed for the Army Nurse Corp. At that time, the army was only offering 1st Lieutenant commissions to nurses who attended three-year nursing programs. I went to a two-year "accelerated" program. For some reason, there was an army policy that only offered two-year nurses the rank of Warrant Officer, not fully commissioned 1st Lieutenant positions. However, it turned out to be great, because Warrant Officer nurses were not required to go to Vietnam, or any other war zone. They were stationed at army hospitals strictly within the continental United States, but still retained all the benefits of fully commissioned officers!

## Report to Fort Sam Houston, San Antonio, Texas

In October of 1966 I was instructed to report to Fort Sam Houston in San Antonio, Texas, for basic training. Two of my friends in nursing school were also drafted, so Dick, Bill, and I packed up and headed off for the long drive from California to Texas in Dick's small VW. I'd never been to Texas before. The trip through the state took forever. We ended up driving through West Texas on the way to San Antonio. That region has to be one of the most remote, driest, flattest places on Earth! Nothing but flat desert land and fences that go on forever. I thought we'd never reach our destination. In fact, the vast desolate wasteland in West Texas prompted me to make up a story about the place. Hope it doesn't offend any of you die-hard residents of the Lone Star State. There are many beautiful places in the state of Texas. However, in my humble opinion, West Texas isn't one of them. Anyway, here's the story.

## Henry and Martha in West Texas

In the early 1800s, a young boy and girl grew up in West Texas just down the road from each other. As they grew older, they fell in love, married, and raised a family. One day Henry said to his wife, "Martha, things are getting pretty tough for us around here. Maybe there's a brighter pasture out there someplace for us. I've never seen what's beyond the horizon, and would like to go out and take a look. Would that be okay with you?" "Sure, Henry, it would be nice if we could find another place with more opportunity, and maybe with some trees!"

So Henry packed up some provisions, mounted Gertrude, the family mule, and headed out. A month passed, and Martha began to worry about Henry's fate. Then one day she saw Henry coming over the horizon. As he approached the homestead, Martha ran to him and embraced his tattered, thin body. She then asked, "Well, what'd you find out there, Henry?" Henry replied, "*Nothing.* It's all like this, and I didn't see one tree. We may as well stay right here!"

## Arrival at Fort Sam Houston

When Bill, Dick, and I got to basic training at Fort Sam Houston in San Antonio, Texas, out of our class of about two hundred, we were the only three Warrant Officers in the entire class! There were some Warrant Officers at other places on the base, but they were all helicopter pilots. Most of the other male nurses in our class were also upset about being drafted. Once they found out about our fortunate situation, they were all asking us, "Hey, how can I become a Warrant Officer? I'm not interested in going to Vietnam, or any other war zone!" But many did end up in war zones.

## *THE GOOD...*continued: Meeting my wife Joan

As young kids, my wife Joan and I lived just a short distance away from each other, and never knew it until years later as adults. Joan was a Navy brat, traveling all over the world with her folks. One place her dad was stationed at was Mare Island Navy Shipyard in Vallejo, California, only a stones throw away from where I grew up. Joan also eventually became a Registered Nurse, and joined the Army Nurse Corp. By fate and God's will, we both ended up at basic training in San Antonio, Texas, at Fort Sam Houston in 1966. We met while cleaning our mess kits one day after lunch.

## Awaiting our assignments

Out of a class of about two hundred, the army assigned only four of us to Valley Forge Hospital in Phoenixville, Pennsylvania. Miraculously, Joan and I were two of the four. I figured, what the heck, my specialty was psychiatry, so after basic training, I'd obviously be assigned to the psychiatric unit at Valley Forge. It made perfect sense, right?....*Wrong!*

Instead I was assigned to an orthopedic ward, a medical discipline I had no experience in! The military usually does everything just the opposite of what you'd expect.

I spent the next two years there. Joan was eventually assigned to an army field hospital in Korat, Thailand. In June of 1968, we both managed to get leave, flew to Honolulu, Hawaii, and were married. We then returned back to our respective assignments for the remainder of our military service.

## *THE BAD:* Life changing injuries and scars

While stationed at Valley Forge during 1966 through 1968, I witnessed first hand the results of the war. Dover Air Force Base was located not far from Valley Forge. Each Wednesday, young men with severe injuries on the battlefield were flown to Dover, then brought directly to the hospital. Patients were then assigned to various wards depending upon the severity of their injuries. The unit I worked on received some of the most severe cases: severed arms and legs, spinal injuries, head and neck trauma, and worse. Many joined to serve, others were drafted, but all had injuries and life changing scars from a cause that ended in defeat and humiliation for the United States.

## *THE UGLY:* Fifty-six thousand lives lost—for what?

Many historical records place the entrance of the United States into the Vietnam conflict around 1959. The conflict ended in April of 1975, when the North Vietnamese captured Saigon, South Vietnam's capital city, now known as Ho Chi Minh City. Ho was the original Vietnamese Communist Revolutionary leader. The event marked a bitter defeat and embarrassment for the United States after a sixteen-year futile attempt to prevent such an occurrence. However, more importantly was the loss of fifty-six thousand American lives, plus countless others injured in what many consider a meaningless and useless effort.

## Service with honor and pride

I know for a fact most young men who served on the battlefield during that time served proudly and with honor. They did their duty, yet sadly upon returning home, they were not looked upon as returning heroes, but rather convenient scapegoats for an angry and war-weary nation during a most turbulent time in history. Fifty-six thousand lives sacrificed, plus thousands more scarred physically and emotionally in a conflict many still view as *ugly* and *useless.*

## *VALLEY FORGE HIGHLIGHTS:*
## Some funny, some not so funny

I'm sure anyone reading the information about my military days at Valley Forge may have found it boring. Clearly understood. Who cares, right? But, if you've got this far and desire to continue, you might find these few experiences interesting. If not, hope you at least found some portions of this book worth reading.

While at Valley Forge, I ran with a bunch of "rebel" officers, who also didn't care for military service, but we all performed our duties as required.

One night while out with my officer buddies drinking, at two in the morning, one Captain said, "Let's go back to base and do a spot inspection of one of the enlisted mens barracks." "Are you kidding Lonnie?" I exclaimed. "No, let's do it," he said. We all tried to pursuade him not to, especially since he had *nothing to do with any of the enlisted barracks*. But he went back and did it anyway, waking up fifty enlisted men at two thirty in the morning, calling a major inspection. Two days later, he would either face a court martial, or be requested to resign his commission. We never saw him again after that!

I worked on the psychiatric unit. Many patients had been in some form of trouble, and were often interviewed by the MP's (Military Police). When entering the psychiatric unit, the MP's had to leave their side arms ( guns ) at the nursing station to be placed in a safe.

One day the MP's arrived and set their guns on a table. I was down the hall and heard the *Bang!* A patient was near the nursing station sweeping floors. The nurse on duty looked away for just a moment before putting the guns in the safe. The patient dropped his broom, ran to the table, grabbed one gun, and blew his brains out right in the nursing station! At the time, my wife-to-be Joan was stationed in Korat, Thailand. She told me she read about the incident in the *Stars & Stripes Military Newspaper* - all the way over there!

Valley Forge also had a great golf course on the base. I played there often and won the "B" Flight Hospital Championship Tournament in 1967.

I also did some evening "moonlight" work at a local hospital to make some extra bucks. One evening I was having dinner with the physician on duty. Dessert was banana cream pie. I ate mine, then he offered me his, since he didn't want it. Why not? So I ate it too. Problem? It was all contaminated! As a result, I developed a severe case of a rare form of salmonella food poisoning.

Next morning, I'm admitted to Valley Forge Hospital, deathly ill. Once they found out what I had, my physician ordered an antibiotic to kill the bug . . . but ordered one that *didn't work*! Not strong enough. Too late! The bug traveled all over my body! I was severely ill for three months in the hospital, beating death on several occasions while fighting through it. Physicians from John Hopkins University in Baltimore, Maryland, were traveling all the way up to Valley Forge just to walk around my bed and study my case. Why? To try to figure out what was *keeping me alive*! Being a nurse, I knew I was in bad shape. Secretly, I got ahold of my medical chart one day and found out just how sick I was.

I finally recoverd, but suffered the consequences of that fight with the reaper for several years therafter. Also, I finally found out why I survived: God was in my corner and it wasn't my time. He had other plans for Joan and I. She was still in Thailand. Every day I wrote a letter to her or made audio tapes I could send her. Knowing we might be together one day kept me going. That plan eventually played out, resulting in our son Toby coming along and six wonderful grandkids from his marriage.

Oh, and one other thing. In the last fifty-two years I've never had a piece of banana cream pie....and never will!

That's enough boring war stories for now.

# Chapter 36

# *WESTWARD HO:*
# *TWENTY-FIVE YEARS LATER*

## Pennsylvania to California

As was noted in Chapter 1, my folks pulled up their New York stakes in 1944 and headed to California with me and my brother, seeking their piece of the American Dream. Ironically, my wife Joan and I were about to embark on a similar adventure. We would now be leaving Pennsylvania, traveling about the same distance to California, and ending up at the same place they originally did. I'm certain we traveled on some of the same roads, leaving our tire marks blanketed over some of theirs left twenty-five years earlier.

After serving her tour of duty in Thailand, Joan returned to the United States, where we were both reunited at Valley Forge and discharged from the army. We then left Pennsylvania in late 1968, and headed to California. I was again employed by the Department of Mental Hygiene at Napa State Hospital. Joan gained employment at a local hospital, where she eventually became head nurse in the coronary care unit. I continued working at the mental institution for a short time, but desired something else. As mentioned earlier in Chapter 34, before being drafted into the army, I had looked into an opportunity with the

Sandoz Pharmaceutical Company, but Vietnam put the kibosh on that. Then one day I recalled my experience years earlier during that shotgun incident covered back in Chapter 33. I thought, *I wonder if I would enjoy being a Probation Officer?* After checking out the qualifications, I realized I met them all in spades, so I contacted the Solano County Probation Department in Fairfield, California, and asked about possible employment. I also applied at the Fresno County Probation Department in Fresno, California, passed all the tests, and was offered a position there. However, in 1970, Solano County had just approved the hiring of two new Deputy Probation Officer positions, and I was hoping to stay in the local area.

I applied for one of the positions, passed all the tests, and was hired. As mentioned earlier in the book, my first supervisor at the Solano County Probation Department was Ken, the same young Probation Officer who had processed my case years earlier in Solano County Superior Court! The judge I ended up working for also just happened to be Judge Tom, the same judge who presided over my case as a juvenile!........Fate and a small world!

Ultimately, I promoted up the ranks to an administrative position in the department.

## Staying out of trouble, Jim?

Interestingly, there's one thing I'll always remember about my experience and relationship with Superior Court Judge Tom while working as a Probation Officer: Often we would meet in the hallway and talk, or ride the elevator together, or have a conversation in his chambers. With this wry grin on his face, he would always end our talks by saying, "By the way, Jim . . . staying out of trouble?"

## Sometime later: The mysterious invitation

Sometime after I left the Probation Department, I received an un-signed hand written letter requesting my presence at a location in San Francisco. The letter simply stated,"Vitally important you attend, please bring this letter with you." I was to arrive at 7:00 PM on a Wednesday night. The letter was signed, "THE JUDGE," but had no return address or phone number to verify its nature. I knew a lot of Judges, but had no idea what this might be about. The letter provided directions to a location in San Francisco. I didn't know anyone in San Francisco at the time, so this not only came as a big surprise, but had an aura of mystery about it as well. Although a bit skeptical, I decided to go and check it out.

It was raining hard that Wednesday evening as I drove to San Francisco. Following the directions provided, I found the house de-scribed in the letter, parked, and walked up to the front door of this large mansion. I rang the doorbell. After a few moments, a butler answered, asking my name and requesting the letter I had received. After giving it to him, he escorted me in, "Please follow me Mr. Orr, the Judge will be here shortly." I thought, "Judge, what the hell is this all about?"

I was then taken into a library room where four other men were seat-ed. "Please make yourself comfortable Mr. Orr, would you like anything to drink?" "No thanks" I replied, the butler responding, "Don't worry, it won't be long." Obviously still curious about the whole situation, I initiated a conversation with the other men in the room. "Anybody have an idea what this is all about?" They responded, "Nope, we have no idea." After about 20 minutes, I jokingly said, "Anyone up for a game of hearts?" At that moment a man came into the room carrying a large box, placing it on a table in the middle of the room. I immediately recognized him. "Good evening gentlemen, I'm certain you're all wondering why you've been invited here tonight." He then opened the large box and said, "Please come look at this." The five of us then got up and walked to the table. Peering into the box, a stark feeling of terror and alarm gripped each of us!................*to be continued.*

# *EPILOGUE*

## Recalling those *American Graffiti* days

At the time this book was published, my wife Joan and I had lived in the Reno, Nevada, area for many years. Reno is well known for many things, but one of its most famous events is *Hot August Nights,* a yearly event celebrating the fabulous *Rock n' Roll 50's & 60's,* featuring star-studded headliners, daily Show 'n' Shines, and a week-long classic car extravaganza like nothing else in the United States. The event also high-lights cruises on Friday and Saturday nights; *Rock n' Roll* bands; doo wop singing groups; classic car shows; and other things reminiscent of those bygone days. Each time I attend, I'm reminded of the great times I had growing up in the Bay Area during that era, experiencing a big dose of those classic *American Graffiti* days.

## The other side of the mountain

I'm now seventy-nine, heading down the other side of the mountain. Can't say my life has been boring. The scars tell the tale, but God, through the healing power of Jesus, has brought me through them all. Two knee surgeries; half blind in left eye from birth; a foot spur surgery; gall bladder surgery; a battle with death in the army; another ten-round battle with the Grim Reaper back in the 80's I finally won; back problems; a melanoma that was successfully removed; a few surgeries for basal cell carcinoma, probably from playing golf a lot out in the sun; leg and foot edema, leg cramps and pain during the night; plus a multitude of diagnostic tests for numerous other maladies over time.

Now, close to finishing this book, I've developed some kind of kidney problem that may finally take me to the mat unless God intervenes again. Lately, it seems I spend half my time in doctors' offices, reading the same books over and over, waiting for my name to be called. Sometimes I even take my own books with me since I've already read most of the ones they have. For some reason, it also seems I recognize the same old farts sitting around these offices each time I visit. Or, how about this? Have you ever noticed most of the magazines in physicians' offices are about *medical problems*? Who wants to read about medical problems when you're in there for one! You're already a bit depressed, right? Now you want to read about the side effects that might occur from a heart transplant? Give me a break!

I'd rather read about golf!

Recently, I got attacked by a swarm of yellow jackets from a nest I opened while doing some work around the house. Stung me right through my gloves, and chased me all the way back into my garage. Guess what? They're way faster than me! Then I developed an infection from a sting that required treatment at a local Urgent Care center. Like it says in the book of Psalms in the Bible, Chapter 34, verse 19, "Many are the afflictions of the righteous, but the Lord delivers him out of them all."

Well, so far he's kept his promise; I'm still here. So, with his help, I guess I'll just keep on trusting and putting my faith in him. Wonder what's next?

## Stayed active - Most of the time

Anyway, as has been obvious in this book, I've tried staying active most of my life. The sport I've enjoyed playing the most as an adult was golf. Had three holes in one over time. I also played some on the PGT Golf Index Tour and the Pepsi Amateur Tour, winning a few championships. Can't imagine playing golf anymore, unless God heals me of this kidney malady. Working in the garden at our home provides some exercise and joy during the spring and summer months. However, I do get tired of the long cold winters up here in the mountains. Always something to complain about, right? So to finish this section out, my prayer now is that God intervenes and heals me of what appears to be a very serious problem. Have no idea where it came from.

I hope you've enjoyed this book. I give God the glory and credit for protecting me all these years, allowing me to still possess some brain power and memories to write about those great early times growing up as a kid and teenager in Vallejo. I'm certain those of you who were of a similar age at the time across America had the same exciting experiences during those fabulous *Rock n' Roll 50's & 60's.* Unfortunately, those of you who weren't there missed what many consider to be the *Best of times in America!*

Oh, and before I forget, one last thought: I think if God pulls me through this kidney thing I'm experiencing, I may try to write another book. Remember this back in Chapter 31?

## Now I know what hot means, mommy!

As I mentioned back in Chapter 31, when we were very young, most of us hung around the kitchen while our moms were cooking. They would say something like "Don't touch that stove, sweetheart! It's hot!" We didn't know what "hot" meant. Most of us believed what our moms told us, but some of us had to touch that stove to see what she meant. Once we touched it and got our pinkies seared, we were instantly converted from believers to *knowers!* We then *knew* what "hot" meant!

## "Believing" in or "Knowing" God - There is a difference!

It's like this: Most people "believe" in God. But there's a *big difference* between *believing* in him….and *knowing* him.

It's going to take a major miracle from the Lord to deliver me from the present physical plague that's fallen upon me. But, I know he's in the miracle-working business. I've experienced them many times before! If that miracle does present itself, with his help, I think I'll make an attempt at writing a book about how people can come to *know* him and his power, having a real personal relationship with him.That might work. I think I'd like a chance at doing that.

*Post Script Dedications*

---

To my wife Joan:

My wife Joan is a true "Saint," a born-again Christian who has put up with the grief I've caused her for over fifty years. I look back on all the years we've spent together and truly regret not heeding her countless words of wisdom and knowledge over time. Wisdom, if followed, would have prevented much of the grief and pain I experienced during our marriage. She's a true Bible-verse, God-loving Proverbs 31:10 woman: "A wife of noble character . . . worth far more than rubies."

**Bodega Bay, California: One of Joan's favorite places**

To my son Toby and daughter Kelly:

The thoughts on the following pages were added not because they relate so greatly to the material in this book. However, when I was about to complete it, they came to me. I felt I should include them with the hope that Toby and Kelly would appreciate what I'm about to share next.

Although not related to the theme of the book, you may find the following information not only entertaining, but also helpful with some of the issues you may be experiencing in your own life. Please consider reading on.

# Post script short story No. 1

## *THE LOST MINE AT LONG CANYON CREEK*

### Dedicated to Toby Orr

## An Old Friend, Fishing Buddy, and Fellow Prospector

In Chapter 36, Solano County California had just approved the hiring of two Deputy Probation Officers in 1970. I was fortunate to be hired for one of the positions. When I first reported for work, I was surprised to see an old friend from high school sitting in the waiting room. Jim was hired for the second position. We reestablished an old friendship, became close friends again, and also good fishing buddies. Jim's adventurous spirit was similar to mine, always looking to explore new horizons. We both had our favorite fishing spots in the mountains of the Golden State. Mine was up in Lassen County on the Feather River. Jim's was in El Dorado County in the Sierras, deep down in the Rubicon River Valley Canyon in a place called Long Canyon Creek.

My spot was fairly accessible, just a lot of walking in the back country mountains. Jim's was in a more dangerous desolate canyon 2,600 feet straight down a mountain in less than a mile. Almost inaccessible, Long Canyon Creek flowed through a deep canyon gorge. The canyon was filled with plenty of poison oak; the stream with plenty of rainbow and brown trout; and one more item....plenty of *rattlesnakes*!

Before I went on my first trip with Jim down to Long Canyon, he shared a rather tragic incident that had occurred there about one year earlier. Two California teachers had ventured into the area in an attempt to reach the bottom. Unfortunately, one of them slipped on the way down and lost his life in the fall. So, again, the trip down required extreme caution.

We'd go to Jim's place often, and stay at a fully equipped camp he originally set up, upgrading it each summer. Stuck in the middle of Gold Country, we even tried our hand at gold panning and underwater dredging, literally carrying all the mining equipment down into the canyon on our backs. Never found much gold during our tough prospecting efforts, but it was a blast and a real fix when we did find some gold flakes.

About half way down the canyon, there was an old abandoned gold mine obliterated from the side of the mountain, possibly the victim of a shaft explosion or cave in. All the mining equipment was still on the site, and maybe a couple of old prospectors' skeletons still inside the shaft.

During the winters, I'd prepare for summer visits to the canyon by filling my back pack with rocks, then walking up and down our stairs to and from our attic preparing my legs for the strenuous trip ahead.

Jim, on the other hand, was six feet five, and one of Napa Valley's top semi-pro competitive tennis players. His legs were always in shape. We continued visiting our camp at Long Canyon for many summers.

As my son Toby got older, he would often ask about going to Long Canyon with me one day, and although I felt it would be too dangerous for him, I took the chance in 1979 when he was eight.

So, we began planning a trip just for the two of us. As a way of closing out this book, I'd like to dedicate this first post script short story to him, and share a little about that trip we made back in 1979. I'll never forget it, and I know he hasn't. He was about to experience the adventure of a lifetime, getting ready to head off into a wilderness laced with danger and intrigue, a trip he had seen his dad trek off to often, but wished he could do the same one day.

Filled with mystery, it would truly be a *Raider's of the Lost Ark* adventure for him. I often look back on that experience and thank God for protecting us both. It was a dangerous place. Taking an eight year old there was not the wisest thing to do, but then I didn't have much wisdom in those days - still don't! But Toby was very excited about it, so his mom and I needed to make a decision. Joan and I had been to Long Canyon once together. She was petrified while there, and thought she would never be able to get out! But, in spite of her trepidation, we both decided I should take Toby there for his first trip.

With that, we'll begin this short story about Toby's journey into the unknown with his dad in the summer of 1979, his first and only trip down to Long Canyon Creek in El Dorado County, California.

Oh, and one more thing: As I mentioned above, my friend Jim and I continued to go to Long Canyon for many summers thereafter, until a dramatic event brought it all to a close. A black bear showed up one day and kicked us out of our camp....*permanently!*

**Toby at our Napa Valley home in California. All ready for the trip to Long Canyon in 1979. Smile on face, pack on back, prospector's hat—game on!**

I can still see Toby's face lit up like a Christmas tree while we planned the trip that summer in 1979, filling up his pack, putting on his hiking shoes and my old miner's hat I let him wear. Then he organized his fishing equipment, getting everything ready. Once packed, we said goodbye to mom and left about midnight, heading up Highway 80, then east into the Sierras across the Forest Hill Ravine near Auburn, California, into the high Sierras.

Still dark, I had to use my high beam lights at times to illuminate the dark road ahead. We made up a a song about the "Head Lights," and sang it as we drove along. As the high beams flashed on and off, we sang, "I got my lights, now my brights, got my lights, now my brights, got my lights, now my brights" on and on, as we barreled into the dark wilderness. On one occasion, Toby got car sick from either the excitement, or just the constant twists and turns in the road. We stopped for him to puke it out, then back in the truck and down the road again.

High in the mountains, we finally reached our destination, a water tank on the side of the road that was our jumping off point. Still pitch dark, we'd sleep in the bed of the truck until dawn. Sleep? Are you kidding?! Couldn't sleep a wink waiting for the sun to come up. Finally, first light. Out of the truck, on with our packs and equipment, then get ready for the two-and-a-half-hour trek straight down 2,600 feet, using ropes, crossing switchbacks, and slipping through rocky crags toward the bottom.

But there was one last important thing to do before we took off. Not only 2,600 feet down, but 2,600 feet straight back up in a couple of days as well! So, we always left a cooler with ice and some drinks at the top waiting for us when we got back to the truck. Never found it where we originally left it, though. It was always thrown someplace else with bear paw claws all over it, but never opened, so our cool drinks were always waiting for us after the hot strenuous trip back to the top.

Finally, we were on our way down. First thing we saw was a small rattlesnake coiled up next to a tree. Yep, we were in Rattlesnake Country! Pass him by, and keep going. After stopping often for some rest and water from a small crystal clear creek, it was down the mountainside again. Two and a half hours later, we were near the bottom. Looking down about five hundred feet, we saw Long Canyon Creek flowing majestically downstream to our right. But there was one more major obstacle to overcome before reaching the bottom and crossing the creek up to our camp. An obstacle my friend Jim and I always felt was the most dangerous of the trip to conquer before achieving victory at the bottom.

Our makeshift trail now came to the edge of a rock precipice sticking out we needed to traverse. While stretching out around it, you'd literally be hanging in mid air on the rock with full pack on, looking straight down at the canyon floor below. One slip could spell disaster. I was very careful to instruct Toby how to traverse the rock and hang on to it!

We both prevailed. Now only five hundred feet to the bottom, then cross the stream to the other side, then up stream about ten minutes to our camp. After wading through the stream flanked on each side by steep granite cliffs, exhausted and spent, we finally reached camp. Off came our packs, throw a couple of ground covers and sleeping bags on the ground, then hit the dirt for some much needed sleep.

After a couple hours of sleep, we were now up and ready for a day of fun and adventure, but needed to do a couple things first: clean up camp, wash all the dishes, pots and pans, lay out the sleeping areas, collect some water from the stream, organize all the equipment, store all the food and staples away for the next two days, plan our menu, then get ready for the fun stuff - fishing, swimming, and a little gold panning!

Our camp was right next to the stream, so we could easily fish sitting in our campsite if we desired, but not for us. Time to grab a few hot dogs and buns to roast for lunch on the trail, then head up stream for some serious angling! After a full day catching all the trout we needed, its back to camp for a little gold panning and a swim in the cool stream around the sun-baked granite rocks. Just down stream where we originally dropped into the canyon was the largest deep green pool in the area with a falls cascading into it. Down the slide we'd go, careening into the deep, cool green water, then back up and do it again. As the sun began to set behind the high canyon walls on each side, every now and then we'd see a rattlesnake slither out from among the rocks to warm itself on a flat granite rock around us. Just stay alert, always keeping our antennas up, keep our distance, and there was no problem with these critters - at least not until we climbed out of the canyon on our last day. Man, were we in for a "Big Time" surprise!

Toby had brought his fishing pole to the big pool, and had to make at least a few casts before returning to camp for the evening. One cast into a deep dark section and *WHAM!* A hefty brown trout struck his Silver Cast Master like a lightning bolt. Suddenly, line began peeling off the spinning reel drag at breakneck speed as the brown made a run for cover. But it was no match for this eight-year-old master angler. After a few minutes fighting, Mr. Brown was had and on a stringer back to camp for dinner with powdered mashed potatoes, zucchini, and the tomatoes brought from our garden at home. Then slam down a little dessert: a ton of M&Ms !

The deep canyon was now becoming darker. Exhausted after a full day of fun in the sun, it was now time to eat dinner, and get ready for the rack. However, unknown to Toby, there were two more surprises he was about to experience that night. One I knew was about to happen from past trips with my friend Jim, the other a new *twist*, not anticipated.

## Daddy Long Legs, Ring Tail Cats

During our trips to the canyon, my friend Jim and I would always hear noise around the campsite late at night that would wake us just after we fell asleep. Obviously, there's always critters around a campsite, especially if there's any small morsels of food around.

But this occurred constantly, every night after we went to bed. One night, we grabbed a flashlight and quickly pointed it in the direction of the noise. To our surprise, we saw a small, cute, little cat-like critter scurry quickly back into the rocks just behind us. It had large bright eyes and a beautiful long bushy tail with black rings around it. It was a Ring Tail Cat.

Back in the Gold Rush 49er days, Ring Tails actually became somewhat of a pet around miners camps. Smaller than a house cat, they're primarily nocturnal with large eyes and upright ears that make it easier for them to navigate and forage in the dark. They use their long tails for balance and are adept climbers.

So, once Jim and I learned about these critters, we decided to try something to really get a good look at them. One night we got a dish, mixed up some sweet Kool-Aid drink, put it in the dish, then after dark placed it on a rock not far from our sleeping bags, and waited. In minutes we heard all this commotion. Quickly turning on our flashlights, all we saw were bushy ring tails sticking out everywhere from the dish of Kool-Aid, like spokes on a bicycle wheel. Ring Tail Cats Galore, lovin' all that sweet nectar. Couldn't keep 'em out of the camp after that, but at least it kept them from walking all over us while were sleeping....most of the time anyway.

So, with that, I decided to pull a little trick on Toby that night and surprise him with an introduction to these old camp buddies he knew nothing about. But first there was that other *twist* mentioned earlier. It would occur with the kid as we just began to lie down for bed that evening. It was a funny event we both remember and still talk about now and then.

Before I laid the Ring Tail Cat episode on Toby, bushed after the long days adventure, he flopped down on his sleeping bag. We never used a tent, just slept straight on the ground. All of a sudden he jumped straight off the ground, like a Saturn Rocket, and yelled out, "What are those things, Dad?!" As he was laying there, a few daddy long leg spiders began creeping around on the ground in front of his face. They were much bigger in the canyon than anyplace else, and must have seemed liked mammoth Star Wars creatures as they lumbered by his face seemingly massing for an attack! "No problem, Toby, just oversized daddy long legs. Shove 'em aside, they won't bother you." "Okay, dad."

Now it was time to spring the Ring Tail Cat scene on the boy. I told him about these old campsite buddies and how we could lure em in to visit us. A bit scared, he asked, "Will they hurt us, dad?" "Not at all, Toby, they're very friendly." "Okay," he responded. We then put the Kool-Aid on a dish and laid it on a rock nearby. Off went the lantern. Now pitch dark, we both held our flashlights ready, Toby's in a death grip with his right hand, his left hand clutching mine with the power of a vise grip!

All of a sudden, the noise. On with the flashlights and there they all were, coiled around the dish of Kool-Aid. Seeing the light, they quickly scurried back into the rocks. Another new experience for the boy he would never forget.

After two days in the canyon, we packed up in the afternoon, secured the camp, and left in time for the two-and-a-half to three-hour climb out to get to the truck before dark. But as mentioned earlier, there was one more dramatic "Big Time" surprise waiting for us as we made the long strenuous climb up the mountain face in the afternoon heat.

## THE "BIG TIME" SURPRISE

As we were hiking out and exhausted, I took another step, and suddenly this knife-wrenching, bloodcurdling *buzz* of a rattlesnake blistered through the air. It felt like it was right in my pocket!

Adrenaline kicked in as I became airborne…. landing ten feet away! I had just stepped on a rattlesnake! I looked back, and it was now chasing my son up the hill! He was running like an Olympic sprinter, and managed to get away as the rattler disappeared in the rocks. Still in shock, but relieved nothing serious occurred, it was back up the mountain face to our next stop.

Halfway up, a section flattened out next to a cool water spring coming directly out of a rock face. Never tasted better water in my life! No matter what type of food we took with us down to Long Canyon, one thing we never forgot was packaged Kool-Aid drink. As we sat there resting, we broke out a couple of packets and mixed them up for a cool

176

sweet refreshing drink. Toby then noticed a couple of poisonous scorpions crawling along the ground next to the spring that he kept a close eye on before the next leg up. Never a dull moment down in Long Canyon!

After a good rest, it was back on with our packs, and up for the final assault to the top. Then we would find our cooler, have a cool drink, then down the road for the long trip home.

## Boulders down the mountainside

But before we get to the truck, there was one last bit of fun to have before leaving, something my friend Jim and I always did near the top each time we made the trip. I wanted Toby to experience it just for the dramatic sound effects and sheer power it displayed. The incline near the top of the hill was at least a forty-five-degree steep grade going straight down. Yep, mostly forty-five degrees straight down . . . and straight up . . . for hundreds of yards! All around were huge boulders on the ground. Simply loosen a large boulder, get it rolling down hill, and wait. As it picked up speed and barreled down hill, it would eventually hit something way off in the distance; a tree, another boulder, a rock face, whatever. When it did, it produced a mammoth, deafeningly loud blast that echoed throughout the canyon. Nothing at the crash site for it to hurt, just some loud crazy fun before ending the trip.

## Cooler still there, but with plenty of bear claw prints on it!

Finally at the top, we eventually found our cooler with bear claw prints all over it, but still secure. We opened it up, had a cool drink, then packed up, leaving with plenty of memories for Toby to share with his mom and friends back home.

But the best thing….we had survived the dangers and perils of Long Canyon to live and breath another day!

## Ever wake up next to a coiled rattlesnake?....I did!

Many fables and yarns abound about rattlesnakes; some true, most myths. Back in the old west, when cowboys hit the rack at night they'd lay a thick rope around their sleeping area to ward off rattlers. The theory was that rattlers wouldn't crawl over the rope, sensing it was a log. If the rope wasn't there, it was felt the snake would seek the warmth of a cowboys body and crawl in with him, leading to big trouble! Other "Rattler" stories surfaced over time, including these. "If you kill a rattler, rub the rattles on your eyes. You'll then "see" the rattler before he see's you." " If you display the rattle of a dead snake, it will keep other rattlers away and act as a charm against a rattlesnake bite." Many other stories and songs about rattlesnakes live on, making the heart throb and the mind bristle with an aura of fear and anxiety. But, here's a story that's actually true. It happened to me on one trip down to "Rattlesnake Country" in Long Canyon many summers ago. I often think about how close I came to being another "Rattlesnake Bite" statistic, and how God protected me from being just that.

The 2600 foot trip down the mountain to the bottom in less than a mile was strenuous on its own. Injecting a 50 lb + pack on your back into the mix made for an even more demanding endeavor. After the two and one half hour trek, we'd finally reach our camp that was right next to the creek. The first thing we did was lay out a sleeping area, then hit the ground for a long nap. Out of habit, I've always slept on my stomach, so I laid down and my fishing buddy Jim hit the ground to my left.

Some time later I woke up still on my stomach, my head turned to the right resting on my hands. There was a tree in our camp, its stump about 5 feet away to the right. We used one of the tree limbs to hang a lantern on. Half asleep, I noticed a bright colored green object on the ground about 3 feet away. It was the lantern wick that had fallen to the ground. Again, in a half asleep stupor, I continued staring at the bright green wick, but then noticed something else. You guessed it....a Coiled Rattlesnake right next to the wick, ready to strike instantly at anything threatening it, and only arms length away from where I was lying!

Normally, if I had been wide awake during such an ordeal, I probably would have panicked and became airborne. Worse yet, and half asleep, at any time I could have extended my right arm out and been bitten instantly. No cell phones then, and no way for a helicopter to get into that narrow canyon. Only one way out and that was straight up for two to three hours. With my heart pounding and venom pumping through my veins, I'd probably be dead half way up the mountain.

Instead, still in a sleep supor, I remember saying something like, "Oh, a rattlesnake." Then slowly rolling to my left and quietly waking Jim up I said, "Jim, we've got a rattler coiled up over here by the tree." "What!" Jim exclaimed. We then eliminated the threat.

My guess is while I was sleeping, either the rattler was slithering down past me to get a drink from the creek, or returning after having a drink. I must have moved in my sleep the instant it got near me. Sensing danger, it immediately coiled up and was ready to Rock n' Roll. Again, God's hand and protection was on me as we experienced another "Routine Day" in Long Canyon....Time to go fishing!

Post script short story No. 2

# *THE FREEDOM OF FORGIVENESS*

## For Kelly

## Should you choose to continue reading on, here's a question to consider:

*Ever have a problem asking for forgiveness or receiving forgiveness in your life?*

Without my daughter Kelly's help, this book would not have been published or printed. Some time ago I told Kelly I had been working on it for a couple of years. She immediately offered to help get it printed, something I was not expecting. The book has basically been something to keep me busy during boring hours, or more lately nights I was awake not feeling well due to a recent serious illness.

I wanted to dedicate this section to Kelly for the help she's provided, but also share a few personal thoughts that may have contributed to a less solid foundation between us, one that could have been much better. Simply put, her mother and I divorced when Kelly was very young.

There's always a "blame game" someplace hanging around to play. I'd be on the losing end of that game all four quarters. However, more importantly, I wanted this section to be about restoration, or rather establishing a new meaningful relationship with my daughter that appears to be occurring more recently. That's what this section is all about.

I recently contracted a very serious kidney illness. Unless God intervenes and heals me of it, looks like I'm in for another ten-round bout with the Grim Reaper. Been in fights many times with this guy. He's always a tough opponent. But, I haven't lost yet and still have the same manager in my corner who knows all of his crafty moves!

In my life, there were probably many factors that contributed to my lacking the effective skills needed as a parent. Not an excuse. I still made all the bad choices. Nobody forced me to choose the destructive roads I've traveled on. I've forgiven my parents for any negative influence they may have had on me. I guess they did the best they could with the tools they were given. But a few things have always troubled me regarding all this. Just felt compelled to share them here. Any reader can simply gloss over them, or don't read any of this at all. Your choice.

It's said parents are usually the ones who lay the parenting skills foundation for their own children, who eventually become parents themselves. I guess we can all make excuses for not being the best parents we could have been. I certainly can. But there are a few things I've always had difficulty with as an adult, battling those *dark alley cats* always trying to get into my house, the ones that try creeping into all of our hearts at times.

Most of his life my dad was an alcoholic. In fact, he died from stomach cancer, so I'm certain alcohol played a role in it. My parents yelled at each other constantly. Mom was what you would call a *co-dependent* of an alcoholic husband, going along for the ride and "tolerating" his aberrant behavior. Apparently she had no idea how it might affect her children, especially the oldest, me. For some reason, I don't think these things affected my brother as much, but they did me. Even to this day, I remember my dad pulling into a bar often, then leaving my mom, brother, and me sitting in the car while he went into the bar to drink, not coming out for extended periods of time.

While I was a teenager, my dad still drank heavily with his two or three drinking partners as they went off someplace. Then while home, if the spirit of alcohol took over, it was yelling, screaming, or throwing things. One time I remember him coming home late with his nose cut halfway open. Drunk on the highway, then off the road in an accident. Not much of an example for his own sons as possible future parental figures.

Unfortunately, most of my young adult thought patterns regarding my father took the form of committing myself to taking steps in my life to *not* be anything like him. Sad scenario, but that was the case. However, isn't it strange that in so many cases, no matter what we do to not emulate some of the negative traits our parents may have exhibited, many of us grow up adopting some of the same negative life style patterns.

So, what does a young person do in such a dysfunctional home? Well, one thing is to continue tolerating it; that is, adopting the same co-dependent behavior as others in the home, or *try to find a way out!*

All of the guys I ran with in the *Slicks Car Club* during those days were older. So, when they became old enough to go into a bar to have a beer, I couldn't. Just needed to go home or someplace else. In addition, most of us still lived with our parents or relatives and couldn't afford to have a place of our own. So many of the guys began talking about doing something else to escape their own dysfunctional families at home. *Hey, what about getting married? That sounds like a fun thing!*

They all started getting married! We were going to weddings almost every month. So, one day I asked Kelly's mom if she wanted to marry me. After all, everyone was doing it. Must be a good thing, right? I felt I loved Kelly's mom, although I probably didn't know what real love was, growing up in the environment I was raised in, but I knew my mom loved me. So, we got engaged, planned a wedding with the folks, and did it. Great foundation to start on, huh? *"Marriage sounds like a fun thing to do."*

Most of us guys were too young, with little or no understanding about what marriage really involved. We were pretty dumb and stupid about that institution in life, other than knowing it wasn't working well with most of our own parents, and was at least one way to get out! So many of the guys in the Slicks Car Club just starting doing it, getting married to their girlfriends.

One day my wife Joan told me Kelly's grandmother told her something about Kelly's mom and I. She said, "Joan, that marriage didn't have a chance from the start!" She was right, and mostly because of me and my selfish desires, plus the homeless heart invaders mentioned below, that I allowed to invade my life and set up housekeeping. So Kelly's mom and I got married, and Kelly came along later. I was working nights, driving to college fifty miles each way during the day, taking stimulants to keep me awake to study, then trying to sleep during the day with earplugs in an attempt to keep the noise out from the German Shepherd dog next door that barked all day long! A recipe for disaster!

Some say time heals most family wounds. Actually, I believe that may be a misnomer. Instead, time often allows certain sinister homeless invaders to move into a persons heart and take up permanent residence, never to leave unless driven out. Who are they? What are their names? Consider a few of them listed here. You'll recognize them.

How about unforgiveness, selfishness, anger, hatred, revenge, bitterness, rebellion, evil plotting, rejection, and even murder? (Not actual physical murder, but certainly murder in the heart toward others that may have hurt us.) These invaders and others are out there lurking and just waiting for the opportunity to take up permanent residence in our hearts.

Allow these buzzards to enter your digs and it's likely they'll take over, rearranging the furniture, turning on the TV, and laying out the chips and salsa for Monday night football. But they're not just looking for homes and hearts to live in. These roving marauders want to move in and *ransack the place!*

Over the years, I've often been tricked into allowing a few of these *black alley cats* to come visit. Their goal? To destroy, divide, maim, and kill. Evil spirits in a dark world of deception and spiritual warfare, clearly described in the Bible, Ephesians, Chapter 6, verses 10 through

18. I've found only one way to truly eradicate them. Oh, they'll always try to sneak back in, and often do, but with this powerful weapon, these cockroaches don't have a chance of remaining around for long. I wish I would have learned about this weapon much earlier in life.

*What's the weapon?*

Well, it's not a gun, knife, or an explosive device you can hold in your hand. It's not the police you call up to arrest these thieves, or the fire department to put out the fire. It's not bear spray, mugger fogger, or pepper spray. It's not poison, green soap, or ant killer. It's not an eraser, and it's not any of those household pest control products found on the shelves of your local home improvement store. Then what is it?

It's *forgiveness . . .* and *. . . faith in God!*

*Forgiveness* - the rarest, hardest, and most effective weapon in the world to use against these culprits, the one weapon that can free us from the burden, hurt, and pain unforgiveness causes. And the best thing about it? It's given to us *free of charge* by God, and doesn't cost a dime! We just need to accept it and use it - and that's where the work begins!

So why is it so hard to *express* forgiveness? Well, because it involves the ultimate sacrifice, giving up ourselves. That is, it requires the same thing God did for us when he freed us from these same brats that continue to plague our lives by sacrificing his only begotten son Jesus. He paid the penalty for those culprits that have plagued lives throughout history, the ultimate sacrifice for our mistakes: *giving up his life for ours!* And in doing so, forgiving us. So, since God made the ultimate sacrifice for us, it makes sense that to be free from the burdens unforgiveness places upon us, we must do the same thing, forgive....not an easy task!

So you see, this closing story is really about *forgiveness* and *restoration.*

A couple of final thoughts: For my wife and I, the ultimate book of truth, wisdom, and spiritual guidance is God's word, the Bible.

However, many of you who have taken the time to read this far may not agree. Clearly understood. Just happens to be what we choose to accept. Over the years, I've also read several books embracing various biblical approaches to dealing with problems in our lives. Many offer sincere attempts at providing solutions to deal with those household bullies that are constantly trying to enter our dwelling, or more specifically, our *hearts*. But I never came across one that addressed the core principle of *unforgiveness* at any depth, at least not until many years ago.

One day I came across this book that got my attention, and with God's help, changed my life. If you've ever had a problem either expressing or receiving *forgiveness*, I'd like to share the name of the book with you. If you're experiencing the trauma and torment of those homeless evil alley cats mentioned earlier, trying to take up permanent residence in your heart, I guarantee the steps outlined in this book will help eliminate them from your life, if you choose to implement them....and that's the big if!

The short paperback book was originally written by David Augsburger in 1970, and revised over the years by the Moody Bible Institute of Chicago. I'm certain it can be ordered on Amazon, or found in any Christian bookstore across America. Its name? Simply, *The "Freedom" of Forgiveness.*

Here's an interesting story to illustrate how it works. Once Billy Graham's wife was flying to some destination. A man seated next to her recognized her and asked, "Aren't you Ruth Graham, Billy Graham's wife?" She responded, "Yes, I am." The man then expressed his admiration for both of them, and the work they did over the years. He then asked: "You've both been married for a long time, haven't you?" "Yes, over sixty years," Ruth replied. The man then said, "My wife and I are having some serious problems right now. Would you mind if I asked you a question?" "Why no, please do," Ruth replied. "Ever have any serious marital problems during all those years, Mrs. Graham?" Ruth replied, "Are you kidding? You think we're not human?! Anyone married for sixty years is bound to have some serious problems between them along the way."

The man then asked this final question: "If you could, what would be the one thing that helped you get through all the problems you might have had in your marriage?" Without hesitating, Ruth replied, "Well, like it says, we all fall short of the glory of God. Most won't agree, but we're all sinners. But God sacrificed his son as a blood offering for our sins, so we can be cleansed and forgiven for our mistakes. . . assuming we do desire to change with his help. Oh, we'll continue to slip now and then. That's life, but God will always be there to help us get back on the right track. That's what true love is all about. So, to answer your question, what would be the one thing that helped Billy and I get through all the serious problems we had? The answer: *Two Forgiving People.* One won't do. It must be *Two*! One doing the asking, the other doing the receiving."

No "asking" allows those heart-dwelling villains to remain. No "receiving" does the same. "Asking" and "Receiving" are the two key ingredients that must be used by both parties in order for God to do his work, ridding us of the culprits that desire to continue ruining our lives. But, we can't do it on our own. Just too difficult. We need God's help in doing so, asking him to help us forgive the other in spite of how they've hurt us, and how angry we feel toward them, and accepting anothers act of forgiveness if that be the case.

Again, as I've dedicated this section of the book to my daughter Kelly, I pray God's act of forgiveness will continue to anchor the foundation of a deeper, loving, and more meaningful relationship between the two of us as we move forward. With that said, I do love my daughter

Kelly, and ask her forgiveness, and her mother's forgiveness as well, for my not being the better father I could have been for so many years.

Until whatever's next!

"And we know that in all things God works for the good of those who love him and have been called according to his purpose."

Romans 8:28